Stacey Demarco

2022 LUNAR

& SEASONAL DIARY

Northern Hemisphere

ROCKPOOL
rockpoolpublishing.co

'Whether the universe is a concourse of atoms, or nature is a system, let this first be established: that I am a part of the whole that is governed by nature; next, that I stand in some intimate connection with other kindred parts.'

MARCUS AURELIUS, STOIC PHILOSOPHER, MEDITATIONS: BOOK 10, 167 ACE

A Rockpool book
P.O. Box 252 Summer Hill
NSW 2130
Australia
rockpoolpublishing.co
Follow us! f ⓘ rockpoolpublishing
Tag your images with #rockpoolpublishing

Published in 2021 by Rockpool Publishing
Copyright text © Stacey Demarco, 2021
Copyright Design © Rockpool Publishing, 2021
Design by Sara Lindberg, Rockpool Publishing
Cover design by Kinga Britschgi
Edited by Lisa Macken
Author photo by Jason Corroto

ISBN 978-1-925946-31-4
Northern hemisphere edition

Printed and bound in China
10 9 8 7 6 5 4 3 2 1

2022 CALENDAR

JANUARY
M	T	W	T	F	S	S
					1	2
3	4	5	6	7	8	9
10	11	12	13	14	15	16
17	18	19	20	21	22	23
24	25	26	27	28	29	30
31						

FEBRUARY
M	T	W	T	F	S	S
	1	2	3	4	5	6
7	8	9	10	11	12	13
14	15	16	17	18	19	20
21	22	23	24	25	26	27
28						

MARCH
M	T	W	T	F	S	S
	1	2	3	4	5	6
7	8	9	10	11	12	13
14	15	16	17	18	19	20
21	22	23	24	25	26	27
28	29	30	31			

APRIL
M	T	W	T	F	S	S
				1	2	3
4	5	6	7	8	9	10
11	12	13	14	15	16	17
18	19	20	21	22	23	24
25	26	27	28	29	30	

MAY
M	T	W	T	F	S	S
						1
2	3	4	5	6	7	8
9	10	11	12	13	14	15
16	17	18	19	20	21	22
23	24	25	26	27	28	29
30	31					

JUNE
M	T	W	T	F	S	S
		1	2	3	4	5
6	7	8	9	10	11	12
13	14	15	16	17	18	19
20	21	22	23	24	25	26
27	28	29	30			

JULY
M	T	W	T	F	S	S
				1	2	3
4	5	6	7	8	9	10
11	12	13	14	15	16	17
18	19	20	21	22	23	24
25	26	27	28	29	30	31

AUGUST
M	T	W	T	F	S	S
1	2	3	4	5	6	7
8	9	10	11	12	13	14
15	16	17	18	19	20	21
22	23	24	25	26	27	28
29	30	31				

SEPTEMBER
M	T	W	T	F	S	S
			1	2	3	4
5	6	7	8	9	10	11
12	13	14	15	16	17	18
19	20	21	22	23	24	25
26	27	28	29	30		

OCTOBER
M	T	W	T	F	S	S
					1	2
3	4	5	6	7	8	9
10	11	12	13	14	15	16
17	18	19	20	21	22	23
24	25	26	27	28	29	30

NOVEMBER
M	T	W	T	F	S	S
	1	2	3	4	5	6
7	8	9	10	11	12	13
14	15	16	17	18	19	20
21	22	23	24	25	26	27
28	29	30				

DECEMBER
M	T	W	T	F	S	S
			1	2	3	4
5	6	7	8	9	10	11
12	13	14	15	16	17	18
19	20	21	22	23	24	25
26	27	28	29	30	31	

ACKNOWLEDGEMENTS

With joy, we are here together again for another flow around the sun and through the moon.

This diary is dedicated to those of you who are flowing through these cycles with the intention of returning to a more harmonious relationship with nature.

My gratitude as always to my husband, Adam, and my agent, Richard Martin, for their support. A thank you to my publisher, Lisa Hanrahan, and her team at Rockpool Publishing, and to Kinga Britschgi for her beautiful cover.

This particular diary is especially for Guinness, my feline companion of 21 years. Rest in power, my friend, and thank you for the absolute joy of your being.

And to the goddess Artemis, She who protects, She who is the embodiment of focus and authenticity: this work is as always part of my devotion to you.

HOW TO USE THIS DIARY

Welcome to a new year and a diary with a difference!

I write this diary well in advance of the year it is intended for. Right now it is late 2020 and it has been a very strange and chaotic year, especially considering the instability caused by the global pandemic and the shakings of other social changes.

It was important to me – actually, vital – to be a steady and calming influence for my family and friends and, yes, to all I came in contact with, especially through my work. This was not always easy, yet what I had in my favour was the grounding influence of the cycles.

Within the crazy maelstrom of change, the moon always rose. It travelled surely from dark to new, all the way to full and back, over and over and over. Every night I could use the moon like a sweet touchstone, knowing that it would change steadily. I could go to the beach and see the tides ebb in and out, flowing and receding to nature's regular and predictable timetable.

A little larger a cycle perhaps, I felt the change of seasons more intimately than before. Being sometimes limited to where I could go, my garden became my only playground and I was able to see the minutiae of the death and rebirth of the seasonal cycle. The Wheel of the Year flowed forward from summer, to fall, to winter to spring and summer again and, yes, it did not fail to give me a clear path no matter how bumpy the conditions.

All these cycles gave me a sense of solidness and comfort. In this situation I saw good and bad, difficult and easy, and that all would pass. This firm foundation of being grounded and connected to nature allowed me the strength and resilience to seek confidence and flexibility within me. In magical terms we could call this a core of power, a core that is hard to impact from the outside. Within that too is the possibility of divine risk, of flowful creation, of precious vulnerability ... and the faith to continue despite what is happening.

This seasonal and lunar diary is designed to help you connect in the same way and of course provides all the timings and information that I believe are the most relevant and effective for modern people to progress themselves and their magic. I have never wanted to get overly complex because I want you to create into this work yourself. All the information in this diary can be used in practical ways as the year progresses and changes from season to season, month to month. The clear marking of dark, new and full moon phases throughout the weeks and a daily update on whether the moon is waxing or waning provides an easy way to keep on top of the most advantageous energetic timings for everything from spellcasting, growing and harvesting plants to balance your body or creating personalised rituals. There is also a deity of the month to learn about and spellcraft to try so you can keep real progression going. At the beginning of each month there is a section for keeping track or your ideas and intentions so you can easily take true action to bring them from thought to reality.

While this diary provides a lot of information to work with for even the most experienced practitioner, it is designed for anyone who wishes to delve into incorporating more joy and connection in their lives in a really solid way.

It is this sacred solidness that enables me to be confident and hopeful. I'll keep writing. I'll dream forward. I'll keep wilfully flowing into what I want to see and focus on it. I'll create into who knows what because I have faith in what I'll be creating from and into. I hope you'll come with me.

Remember: you are the magic. You.

Show your power!

With great love

Stacey Demarco

THE MODERN WITCH

STARTING YOUR
YEAR POSITIVELY

Many people decide they won't even try for new year's intentions any more because they can never keep them. Some people do set unreasonable goals (such as losing huge amounts of weight in one month), but the big reason we don't achieve what we say we want is that, really, we don't want it all that badly.

'I do want it, though!' you might say. 'But I really do want to get healthy, or I really do want that new car/house/job/love!' Here is the big reason why you may not want it all that much: because right now it either doesn't align with your values or you want goals that actually belong to someone else. You simply aren't that devoted or you get distracted.

For some people there is the feeling of: 'What if I get this thing, what then? Will my family still love me? Will this new job actually be better? Will my life change so much that I can't control it any more?'

Take all of that and look at it, feel it. That smells like confusion and fear to me!

To assist you to get clearer about what you *really* want, below is an exercise I get participants in my infamous new year's workshops to do. Fill this out before you do any new year's spells or rituals, and I think you may find you get a big truth bomb hitting you in a very good way. You'll sort out what really matters to you, and you can base your resolutions on that and be devoted to what you want to be rather than what you might unconsciously be doing. You'll be able to track your progress and update it as you grow each month on the month header pages.

I love the gateway of the new year because it is a gateway into a fresh start if you wish it to be so. It's a catalyst for change. Many ancient cultures saw the beginning of a new year as an opportunity to journey through a gateway into something unknown, but to do so required a leap of faith both literally and figuratively.

The Romans, for example, took this idea literally, creating new year's doorways dedicated to the goddess Jana and the god Janus that people jumped though from one side to another to signify they had indeed left the energy of the previous year behind and fully accepted a new start. The Mayans smashed statues within gateways representing the old year then walked over the rubble to get to the new year gateway.

We can all jump through a new gateway. We can all be brave and courageous and inspired. We can all be leaders and heroes and have happy endings in our own story. So let us begin . . .

GETTING CLEAR ABOUT 2022

Here are some great questions to ask yourself to get clear about what you want for 2022:

- What are my values? (Values are guiding ideals and principles. Examples of values include honesty, compassion, creativity, calmness, fairness, independence and freedom.)

  _____

  _____

- What are my needs? (Needs are things you must have to be at your best.)

  _____

  _____

- What am I devoted to right now? (You can be devoted to things that are positive or non-positive. You are devoted to what you actually do, for example, if you eat a lot of potato chips then you are devoted to eating potato chips.)

  _____

  _____

- What do I want to be devoted to?

  _____

  _____

- Take those values and needs and think about what would give you the greatest pleasure in 2022.

  _____

  _____

Let's get even clearer by discerning further based on your values and real pleasures:

◆ What would I definitely wish to leave behind in 2021? (For example, think about old patterns, negative experiences, bad habits, ill health and so on.)

_____

◆ Based on my values and pleasures, what would I love to experience but haven't as yet?

_____

◆ If I could make one positive intention for the community or planet as a whole it would be:

_____

◆ Taking all of this into consideration, the new year's intentions I would love to set are:

_____

◆ My intentions for 2022, stated in January, are:

_____

◆ The steps I will take in January are:

_____

◆ The steps I will take in February are:

_____

◆ The steps I will take in March are:

_____

◆ The steps I will take in April are:

_____

◆ The steps I will take in May are:

◆ The steps I will take in June are:

◆ The steps I will take in July are:

◆ The steps I will take in August are:

◆ The steps I will take in September are:

◆ The steps I will take in October are:

◆ The steps I will take in November are:

◆ The steps I will take in December are:

THE NEW YEAR'S
GATEWAY JUMP

Long-time readers of this diary have shared with me how much they love doing the new year's gateway jump. The ancient Romans obviously loved it too, this leaping through the gateway of the new year with the goddess Jana and the god Janus, after whom the month of January was named.

This is a fun ritual to do alone or with friends. There are many different versions of the ritual but all of them involve a physical jump, which I think kick-starts our mind and spirit.

Ahead of time, find a gateway to jump through. Doorways or gates are perfect, or you can create your own by stretching some pretty fabric between two trees at least 1 metre above head level or by drawing a line in the sand.

Gather together:

- some incense and a bowl
- a piece of chalk or a ribbon to mark the gateway jump
- a silver candle and a gold candle
- a bowl of water with two handfuls of salt added
- your list of intentions for the new year of 2022

Go to the location of your new year's jump. Burn the incense in a bowl and allow the smoke to purify the area. You might thank the genus loci (the friendly spirits) of the place for their help. When you are done, draw a line with the chalk or place a ribbon across the threshold of the gate or doorway.

Light the silver candle and say: 'Jana of the gateway, goddess of what was and what will be: I am ready to step through 2021 into this brand new creative possibility of 2022. I have thought about my desires and ask you to grant my intentions if they be for the good of all!'

Light the gold candle and say: 'Janus of the gateway, god of what is behind me and what is in front of me: I am ready to leap excitedly into the future of 2022. Help me achieve my intentions and so much more if it be for the good of all!'

Place your hands in the bowl of salted water and say: 'In your presence I clear away any burdens or poor actions. I cleanse away my fears and doubts and any obstacles in the way of this new year!'

Wash your hands, imagining all negative things in your life being cleansed. Read out your intentions for 2022 three times. Be excited about these intentions: don't be shy! Feel that excitement ripple right through your body.

Step towards the gateway or threshold and say in a clear voice: 'Jana and Janus, take me through the gateway easily and with your protection. I step forward into the new!' Step or jump confidently forward through the gateway.

Say: 'Thank you! Yes!' and clap three times loudly.

Thank Janus and Jana and ask: 'What do I do next?' Listen for any messages or ideas and act upon them as soon as you can.

Blow out the candles after midnight if possible. Throw the salted water down the drain.

Happy New Year, fellow jumpers!

SPELLCRAFT

How and why do spells work?

This is a big question that can be answered! For a detailed explanation read the relevant chapter in my book *Witch in the Boardroom*, but the short answer depends on whether you wish to go the spiritual or scientific route — or both!

THE SPIRITUAL PATH

Witches and those from many other spiritual paths believe we are connected to all things, including the divine. The divine assists us to achieve our intentions through effectively communicating what it is we do or don't want. To perform spellcraft we need to clearly state our intentions and raise considerable energy around the intentions before releasing them in a directed fashion. We then take steps towards what we need and desire and the divine meets us more than halfway. Magic happens; we get what we want.

THE SCIENTIFIC PATH

Spells speak the language of the subconscious, the part of the mind that directs us towards our goals and dreams. It's where ideas pop up and where creativity is based. You can program your subconscious to focus on what you want through elements such as symbology, movement, visualisation and emotion, and spells are a great way to do this effectively.

Whichever path you choose, know that spells, rituals and invocations do work effectively.

FIVE TOP CASTING TIPS

1. Relax and have fun! One of the best ways to ensure powerful spellcraft is to leave all your administration, worries and preconceived ideas behind and just let go. Spellcraft is meant to be a joyful practice; even when casting to rid ourselves of something we no longer need there is at least a feeling of satisfaction or hope that things will change for the better.

2. Don't worry if things don't go perfectly. So what if the candle blows out or the incense doesn't light or your phone rings: does that mean your spell is ruined? Well, only if you stop! Spells are more about knowing what you want and raising power behind this than whether or not things run perfectly. Be confident, hold your intention clearly and keep going.

3. Plan in advance and be clear about your intention. A quickly planned spell can be a good spell but plan ahead when you can, especially when it comes to timing. This diary gives you great timing information to pinpoint the best days to cast for your particular needs. Ensuring you have any ingredients or supplies ahead of time will reduce your stress levels and leave you free to concentrate on your intentions.

I also think it's important to plan for safety, for example, keeping children and animals away from flames, using good-quality magical supplies (which you may have to order) and having the room well ventilated when using incense. Most important, though, is being crystal clear about what you are casting for, as your intention is of utmost importance. (If you don't know what you want you can cast for clarity.) Take time before casting to examine what you do or don't want and put this in clear, concise language. After all, if you don't know what you want the universe can't co-create properly with you.

4. Don't interfere with free will. It is a terrible misconception that witchcraft is commonly used to directly control the mind or actions of other people, when in fact one of the key tenets of most witchcraft traditions is to never interfere with another's free will. Spellcraft works very effectively, so it is not fair to impose our own will or what we believe is the best thing for someone else upon another person or cast on or for other people, as it may have consequences. Even if someone is ill, I always ask permission before commencing any kind of healing invocation. If they are very ill and can't give permission I always add the direction 'If it be for the good of all' as a kind of insurance policy.

Love spells are probably the trickiest when it comes to ensuring free will is intact. No matter what, we never cast for a particular person; instead, we cast for the kind of relationship and partner we desire. This means we attract the best candidate, who may or may not be someone we know!

5. Participate! Participating after the spell is a very important aspect of spellcasting, as it is a chance to get moving in the direction of your intention. After a spell is almost complete I always like to ask the divine for their suggestions on what to do next. This request is not answered in a big booming voice that clearly tells me what to do; instead, it comes effortlessly and easily as ideas do, like a popping into your head feeling. By actioning any or all of these messages we are co-creating with the divine and we start moving. Even a small start has a ripple effect that will lead you more quickly to your intention.

SPELLCASTING MADE EASY

Everyone can spellcast! The spellcasting template below will assist you to write your own effective spell. Each spell has a 'skeleton', or a structure that gives the spell form and function, so fill in the template and you'll have the beginnings of a great spell. And remember: be creative and confident and have fun!

Focus: you have decided to cast a spell for a specific reason and begin to plan the process, taking into consideration time and ethics; it can include a list of things you'll need to cast the spell.

Purpose and intention: clearly and concisely state what the spell is for and what you hope to manifest, such as 'Great goddess, I am here to ask you to help me achieve . . . quickly and easily' or 'Universe, I wish to attract my ideal partner for a committed relationship leading to marriage.'

Raising power: raise energy to boost your intention; common ways are raising emotion, meditation, drumming, dancing and moving.

Release: release and send out all the power you have raised into the universe; it should be different from how you have raised power such as burning something, clapping, shouting or stopping the movement suddenly.

Participation and grounding: you may feel filled with energy after casting and wish to ground that energy a little in the physical world. Great ways to do this are to have a bath or shower, place your hands on the ground or on a plant or eat something.

THE MOON'S CYCLES AND PHASES

One of the most common questions around spellcasting is: 'What is the best time to cast my spells?'

The simple answer is *any time*, although certain times are more powerful than others; if we align ourselves with them they can assist us in achieving greater success. As we honour the earth and creation we closely observe and are guided by the cycles of nature, including moon cycles, seasonal changes and the position of the sun in the sky.

Traditionally, witches and pagans work closely with moon energy, which encompasses both moon phases and the tides. This diary gives you clear information about moon phases and also offers suggestions about what to cast for. You can check tidal information with your local newspaper, weather channel or specialist website (see the Resources section at the end of this diary).

MOON PHASE TIMINGS 2022

DARK MOON	NEW MOON	FULL MOON
1 January	2 January, 1.33 pm	17 January, 6.48 pm
31 January	1 February, 12.46 am	16 February, 11.56 am
1 March	2 March, 12.34 pm	18 March, 3.17 am
31 March	1 April, 2.24 am	16 April, 2.55 pm
29 April	30 April, 4.28 pm	16 May, 12.14 am
29 May	30 May, 7.30 am	14 June, 7.51 am
27 June	28 June, 10.52 pm	13 July, 2.37 pm
27 July	28 July, 1.54 pm	11 August, 9.35 pm
26 August	27 August, 4.17 am	10 September, 5.59 am
24 September	25 September, 5.54 pm	9 October, 4.54 pm
24 October	25 October, 6.48 am	8 November, 6.02 am
22 November	23 November, 5.57 pm	7 December, 11.08 pm
22 December	23 December, 5.16 am	

- All times are US Eastern Standard Time.
- Time is adjusted for daylight savings time when applicable; adjust for your state/ country.
- Dates are based on the Gregorian calendar.

SPECIAL MOON EVENTS
- Super new moon: 2 January.
- Black moon (a second new moon in a single calendar month): 30 April.
- Super full moon: 14 June.
- Micro new moon: 28 June.
- Super full moon: 13 July.
- Total lunar eclipse visible in NY: 8 November.
- Super new moon: 23 December.
- Blue moon (the third new moon in a season with four new moons): none for 2022.

WHAT THE MOON PHASES MEAN

Here is some useful information on what each moon phase means for you in terms of energy, as well as some suggestions on what to cast and when.

FULL MOON
- The moon is full in the sky.
- Full energy! Big energy! Kapow!
- This moon gives you high-impact results and is perfect for attraction spells of any type.
- It's a great time to explore and find your true path and purpose in life.
- Witches formally celebrate their relationship with the divine once every 28 days during full moon. This is called an *esbat*, literally a meeting with others in a coven or simply with the divine.

WANING MOON
- The moon is growing smaller in the sky, which occurs between the full moon and the new moon.
- Energy is reduced.
- It's a good time to perform spells with a purpose and intention of getting rid of something that no longer serves you or to reduce an obstacle.
- It's a great time to give up a bad habit such as an addiction or a limiting or negative belief.

DARK MOON
- No moon is visible in the sky.
- This is traditionally a time of introversion and rest.
- It's a good time for spells that ask for peace and creative flow.
- Experienced witches can use this moon for powerful healing through positive hexing.

New moon

- This occurs the day after the dark moon and is good for fresh starts and renewal.
- This is traditionally the time to make seven wishes.
- It is a great time for spells of health and for the beginning of projects or businesses.
- It's a powerful time to cast spells for better mental health.

Waxing moon

- The moon is growing larger in the sky, which happens between the new moon and the full moon.
- Energy is growing and expanding.
- It's a good time to perform spells with a purpose and intention of growth and moving towards something you desire.
- It's a powerful time to ask for more money, more positive relationships and better health.
- Wonderful for prosperity spells.
- Perfect for asking for bodily vitality, a pay rise, a new job or more recognition.

TIDES

As most people know, tides are linked to the moon. The rise and fall of the tides can be used as additional elements in your spells; aligning them with your spells can make the spells even more powerful. Being by the sea or water and seeing the tides ebb and flow will always add an extra dimension to your spell or ritual.

High tide

- This tide brings things towards you, and is known for attraction.
- It's wonderful for prosperity spells.
- It's perfect for asking for better health, a pay rise, a new job or more recognition.

Low tide

- This tide removes things, takes things away.
- It's perfect for removing obstacles, negative feelings, pain, bad memories and office politics.

King tide

- These are very high and low tides that happen on a regular basis.
- Energies are even more emphasised, so make sure what you are asking for is what you truly desire.
- It may be worth 'saving up' a desire for a king tide if it is a request that can wait.

ASTROLOGICAL CORRESPONDENCES FOR KEY MOON PHASES 2022

MONTH	ASTROLOGICAL SIGN	NEW MOON	FULL MOON
January	Capricorn	2 January, 1.33 pm	
	Cancer		17 January, 6.48 pm
February	Aquarius	1 February, 12.46 am	
	Leo		16 February, 11.56 am
March	Pisces	2 March, 12.34 pm	
	Virgo		18 March, 3.17 am
April	Aries	1 April, 2.24 am	
	Libra		16 April, 2.55 pm
May	Taurus	30 April, 4.28 pm	
	Scorpio		16 May, 12.14 am
	Gemini	30 May, 7.30 am	
June	Sagittarius		14 June, 7.51 am
	Cancer	28 June, 10.52 pm	
July	Capricorn		13 July, 2.37 pm
	Leo	28 July, 1.54 pm	
August	Aquarius		11 August, 9.35 pm
	Virgo	27 August, 4.17 am	
September	Pisces		10 September, 5.59 am
	Libra	25 September, 5.54 pm	
October	Aries		9 October, 4.54 pm
	Scorpio	25 October, 6.48 am	
November	Taurus		8 November, 6.02 am
	Sagittarius	23 November, 5.57 pm	
December	Gemini		7 December, 11.08 pm
	Capricorn	23 December, 5.16 am	

THE MOON'S TRANSITS WITHIN ASTROLOGICAL SIGNS

Separate to the meanings of the phases of the moon and the timings of the Wheel of the Year, there is an added layer of meaning where the moon is transiting within the signs of the zodiac. The moon makes a full transit of the earth and the signs every two and a half days.

Listed below are the astrological phases of the moon and some corresponding themes around which magical workings can be performed very effectively.

CAPRICORN

When the moon is in Capricorn it is an excellent time for magic concerning planning, clarity, strategy, career and purpose, status and obstacle busting.

AQUARIUS

When the moon is in Aquarius it is an excellent time for magical workings concerning popularity, strengthening friendships, change, creativity, science and deepening spirituality and for the greater good.

PISCES

When the moon is in Pisces it is a beneficial time for magical workings concerning dreams, completion, increasing psychic ability and intuition and flow. It is also a good time to do healing work around women's cycles.

ARIES

When the moon is in Aries it is a beneficial time for magical workings concerning stamina, leadership, dealing with authority figures, strength and study.

TAURUS

When the moon is in Taurus it is an excellent time for magical workings concerning family and children, love, home matters, the purchase of real estate and creating sacred space in the home.

GEMINI

When the moon is in Gemini it is a great time for magical workings concerning expansion, communication of all kinds, travel, writing and invocations.

CANCER

When the moon is in Cancer it is a great time for magical workings concerning all kinds of emotional healing and cutting cords of old relationships. It is also an optimum time for healing the body and promoting health, particularly through diet.

LEO

When the moon is in Leo it is an excellent time for magical workings concerning self-esteem, personal power, status, authority of all kinds and improving your relationship with your boss.

VIRGO

When the moon is in Virgo it is a beneficial time for magical workings concerning getting or keeping a job, exams, purification, clearing and detoxing of all kinds.

LIBRA

When the moon is in Libra it is an excellent time for magical workings concerning balance, justice, all legal matters, better health and weight balance.

SCORPIO

When the moon is in Scorpio it is a great time for magical workings concerning all sexual matters, healing trauma, reducing gossip and increasing fun.

SAGITTARIUS

When the moon is in Sagittarius it is an excellent time for magical workings concerning truth, clarity, exposing dishonesty and asking for increased travel or protection during travel.

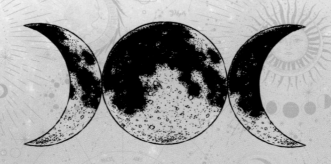

BENEFICIAL TIMINGS

DAWN

- New beginnings.
- New projects.
- Creativity spells.
- Initiations.

SUNSET

- Completions.
- Asking for help for a project or issue that may be long or difficult.
- Spells for faith and preparation.

MIDDAY

- Asking for increased personal power.
- Asking for confidence and strength.
- Asking for the courage to allow your light to shine.
- Worshipping during fire festivals such as Litha.

MIDNIGHT

- The witching hour.
- Asking for self-knowledge.
- Asking for deep and lasting change.
- Asking for help from your ancestors.
- Turning dreams into reality.

EQUINOX AND SOLSTICE UNIVERSAL TIMINGS (UTC)

- Fall equinox (Mabon), 20 March, 15.33 UTC
- Winter solstice (Yule), 21 June, 09.13 UTC
- Spring equinox (Ostara), 23 September, 01.03 UTC
- Summer solstice (Litha), 21 December, 03.27 UTC

EQUINOX AND SOLSTICE EST/EDT (DAYLIGHT SAVINGS ADJUSTED) TIMINGS

- Spring equinox (Ostara), 20 March, 11.33 am EDT
- Summer solstice (Litha), 21 June, 5.13 am EDT
- Fall equinox (Mabon), 22 September, 9.03 pm EDT
- Winter solstice (Yule), 21 December, 4.48 pm EST

ELEMENTS AND DIRECTIONS

You might wish to utilise the elements and directions in your spells and workings to give yet another layer of powerful symbology and energy. Experienced witches use a compass if they are not sure of the directions when setting up a circle; you may even find one within your mobile phone.

Here are some suggestions for ways of honouring each direction along with its corresponding element, but ultimately the combinations are up to you and will depend on the surrounding geography. There used to be very strict correspondences highly influenced by the northern hemisphere; however, pagans and witches all over the world now combine the elements and directions in the way that the surrounding geography most calls for. So, for example, if you were standing facing east in Sydney, Australia the dominant element in the environment would be the ocean (water), so I cast east as water.

NORTH/EARTH

- Salt, earth, oils such as oak moss, patchouli.
- Standing on earth, sprinkling of earth and salt, anointing stones.
- Represents resilience, order, law, politics, education, security, money.
- Green/brown.
- Night.

SOUTH/FIRE

- Candles, open flame of any kind, oils such as pepper, ginger, frankincense.
- Lighting flame, passing flame around the circle, anointing with oil.
- Represents passion, purpose, strength, achievement, destruction of what is not needed.
- Masculine: sun.
- Red.
- Noon.

EAST/AIR

- ◆ Incense, fragrance, smoke, kites, balloons, oils such as bergamot, lime, eucalyptus.
- ◆ Smudging, blowing smoke, bubbles, bells, singing bowls.
- ◆ Represents communication, creativity, logic, travel, new beginnings, ideas, flow.
- ◆ Yellow.
- ◆ Dawn.

WEST/WATER

- ◆ Salt water, moon water, shells, rain, oils such as rose, ylang ylang.
- ◆ Anointing with water, passing the cup.
- ◆ Represents relationships, love, psychic connection, birth/death/rebirth.
- ◆ Feminine: moon.
- ◆ Blue.

WHEEL OF THE YEAR

As the path of the witch is an earth-based faith, the witches' sabbats or holidays are intrinsically connected to the cycles of nature. Primarily, the themes of birth, death and rebirth are played out across a year that is divided into light and dark, male and female, sun and moon, growth and rest and heat and cold.

It is important then to understand that the traditional Wheel of the Year timings are reflective of the northern hemisphere cycles and for those folks in the southern hemisphere, we flip the timings according to the way seasons flow to keep rhythm with that environment. For this northern hemisphere diary, I have aligned the celebrations along traditional northern hemisphere dates.

Importantly, these sacred times connect you with the light, land and seasons. The land is our mother; she feeds us, shelters us and gives us comfort and joy. The festivals give us a chance to give something back to her and honour all that she does. As modern people we often forget this and feel disconnected without quite knowing why.

The continuous cycle of nature lends itself to the image of a wheel. The ancient Celts and their predecessors saw time as a wheel or as a spiral divided by eight festivals, listed below. Modern witches can use the themes of each celebration to do magical workings of their own in complete synergy with the natural cycles. The dates featured on solstices/equinoxes are to be used as a guide only, so please refer to the diary itself for accuracy.

Note: Where these festivals fall within the calendar spreads within this diary I have given further information on the festival and some suggestions about how to celebrate the Sabbath with meaning.

SAMHAIN (HALLOWEEN)

- Southern hemisphere 30 April; northern hemisphere 31 October
- Celebration of death as a continuation of life
- Borders between the dead and living are not fixed and impassable
- The veils between the worlds are at their thinnest so one can ask the ancestors and spirits for guidance and communication on the future
- Celebrating where you came from
- Traditional time for scrying
- Witches' new year!

YULE (WINTER SOLSTICE)

- Southern hemisphere 21-23 June; northern hemisphere 21-23 December
- Longest night of the year
- Mid-winter festival linked to the Christian Christmas
- Archetypally linked with the birth of a child of promise and light: Dionysus, Arthur, Jesus, Baldur
- Celebrates the return of the sun and thus hope
- Abundance spells and charms
- Giving thanks and gifts of goodwill

IMBOLC (CANDLEMAS)

- Southern hemisphere 1 August; northern hemisphere 1 February
- Celebration of light returning
- Goddess as Brigid (St Brigid)
- Fire festival
- Clarity and healing
- Light to shine, self-knowledge/creation

OSTARA (SPRING EQUINOX)

- Southern hemisphere 21-23 September; northern hemisphere 21-23 March
- Night and day are equal, but moving towards summer
- Balance and growth
- Leave what you don't want and create the new
- Fertility and love
- New projects

BELTAINE (MAY DAY)

- Southern hemisphere 31 October; northern hemisphere 30 April/1 May
- Marriage of the goddess and the god
- Maypoles, phallic and yonic symbolism
- Love magic (weddings/hand fastings)
- Animus and anima/masculine and feminine balances

LITHA (SUMMER SOLSTICE)

- Southern hemisphere 21-23 December; northern hemisphere 21-23 June
- Longest day, shortest night
- Sun is at its fullest power yet the year begins to wane from here
- What brings light and joy into your life and develops this
- Self-development
- Celebration of the masculine divine

LAMMAS (LUGHNASADH)

- Southern hemisphere 1 February; northern hemisphere 1 August
- First harvest, first loaf baked
- The god begins his journey into the underworld
- Sorrow and celebration
- Fruition, taking stock and harvesting what you have achieved

MABON (FALL EQUINOX)

- Southern hemisphere 21-22 March; northern hemisphere 21-22 September
- Harvesting the main crop
- Take stock of what has served you well and what has not
- What needs repairing before the dark comes
- Preparation for harder times
- Welcoming change energy

THE MOON AND
YOUR BODY

We are moon-influenced animals even if most of us don't go howling under it! Long-held knowledge indicates a number of ways the moon can impact our physical bodies.

DETOXING

Many of us at some stage feel the need to re-energise the body through a detox of some sort. Usually it's after a period of overindulgence: perhaps too much rich food, alcohol or sugar. Detoxes became quite fashionable and all kinds of weird and wacky systems and products are now being promoted. I am not a big fan of detoxing in its newest, most faddish form, but if a detox to you means a period of consuming more deeply nourishing food in smaller quantities, less stimulants and alcohol and more sleep, I am all for it!

Should you decide a detox is something you do wish to undertake, the moon can help you make this time more successful.

One-day detoxes: early on the day before a new moon (dark moon), set an intention that over the next 24 hours you will release what your body does not need. Upon waking on the new moon day, set an intention to release all that you don't need and start your detox.

Longer detoxes: begin your program on a full moon, setting an intention that as the moon wanes so will the toxins be released from your body. Continue your program during the waning period but no longer.

Note: unless you are sure you are fit enough to embark on a detox program, do not attempt to do it yourself. Seek professional advice.

WEIGHT BALANCE

Setting your intention and beginning your healthy weight program on a **full moon** is a great idea as it gets your mind used to the idea that this is something you want. You might even cast a spell for health and vitality that night to boost it along. (There is a good spell free on my website www.themodernwitch.com.)

Begin your program straight after a full moon and notice that the moon is **waning**, taking with it extra weight and fluid. You will lose more weight more rapidly during a waning moon.

When the moon becomes a **new moon** you should do another ritual to boost your intention. Lighting a candle and simply asking the universe to continue to assist you to reach your goal and achieve greater health is enough.

You must be careful not to eat foods during a **waxing moon** cycle that are not aligned with your intention, as these cycles will hold them to the body far more than during waning cycles. However, you will generally have more energy during waxing moons so this is the time to boost your activity levels and burn off what you consume more easily.

When the moon becomes **full** again, be grateful for what you have achieved or achieved so far and set your intention moving forward.

HAIR

I know many lunartics love cutting and growing their hair by the moon cycles, and I also know that full and new moon days are some of the most popular days in hairdressers all over the world! It is thought that different phases influence hair growth just as they influence tides, so it's no surprise that full and waxing moons are best friends to those of us who want longer locks.

Growing your hair: traditionally, should you wish to grow your hair cut it only when it is in its most active phase during a full or waxing moon.

Keeping your hair a similar length: if you wish to preserve your haircut, which is very handy for those who have a fringe or short hair, cut your hair on a waning moon.

Strengthening your hair: try new moon days and waxing moons to apply treatments to your hair.

For the mother of all good hair days go for a full moon in Cancer for all your conditioning and cutting treatments.

Hair removal: whether you wax, laser or shave, the best time to remove hair is during a waning moon cycle. It will stay away for longer.

BALANCING BODY CYCLES

There is some excellent research available on the correlation of lunar light, moon phases and bodily biorhythms such as those related to our hormonal and fertility cycles. There seem to be two camps on this: one that sees no correlation with the moon cycles of 28-29 days with the typical female cycle of the same length or with a spike in fertility around the full moon, and another that recognises this long-held wisdom as fact.

If you have a menstrual cycle that is radically less or more than 29 days you may consider it beneficial to balance your cycle. To do this, watch the moon for five minutes each night. You need light to activate a whole cascade of bodily functions, and the fertility cycle is but one of them. If you wish, you could visualise your most fertile time at a full moon (full power!) and your wise blood flowing around a dark/new moon (letting go, starting afresh).

THE LUNAR RETURN

Across a number of ancient cultures such as the Egyptian and Sumerian it was believed the moon phase upon birth triggered the beginning of life and remained as a person's peak time energetically throughout life. This was especially evident for women, as it determined their most fertile time. Sumerian medicine records indicate a belief that a woman was most fertile when the moon was at the same phase as her birth. Ancient Celts and Egyptians recorded the moon phase at birth and told both sexes when they came of age. This is called a lunar return.

A lunar return is not what astrological moon sign you were born in; it's more astronomy than astrology! Rather, it's what actual phase was in the sky upon your birth; for example, full moon, quarter moon, two days before a new moon and so on.

Until fairly recently the accepted science was that women had a covert cycle of ovulation. This referred to a hidden set time, usually at the centre of the cycle, but with no overt obvious clues such as your cat or dog might display when on heat. Science indicated there was only one small fertile time in a human woman's cycle and that it had to be around that centre point. However, there have been some recent studies that indicate the contrary: that a lot of exposure to sex/men can cause spontaneous ovulation at any time in the month. Further studies are now being undertaken to see if there is any pattern to this within diet and light exposure. Perhaps in this case old wisdom is true wisdom!

If you are male this also includes you. Scientists believe men have a fertility biorhythm and it could well be related to light and frequency of sex.

The simple idea of knowing which phase of the moon you were born during as well as keeping an eye on the moon regularly seems to induce more hormonal balance in both sexes, and is very useful if you are wishing to conceive (or not). If you are interested in more thorough information about the moon and fertility and how to best take advantage of this you might like to read my book *Witch in the Bedroom*.

Wouldn't you like to know when you are physically and mentally at your best, or when you are at the top of your game for sport, exams or decision-making? Knowing when you will be feeling most vital and energetic really does have profound impacts on everyday life.

LUNAR/SOLAR ENERGY AND CRYSTALS

Utilising crystals to focus and capture energy is something that both pagan and non-pagan practitioners do. One of the most popular ways of cleansing and charging your crystals is to place them under the moonlight. However, there are some subtle ways of enhancing crystal energy by matching the specific lunar energy at certain times in the cycle or by using solar energy.

LUNAR ENERGY

Cleansing: leave your crystals out under the power of a full or waxing moon. If you are using the powers of a waxing moon, leave the crystals out on multiple nights right up to the full moon.

Dedicating for matters of prosperity: I have had success with leaving crystals in a bowl of shallow water out in the moonlight. The water promotes the flow of money towards you.

Dedicating for matters of growth: place your crystals on living soil or a plant. Grass is perfect, as is a healthy pot plant. Leave the crystals out under moonlight and then leave them out for a full day of sunshine as well.

Dedicating to absorb negative energies: many crystals are useful to us in the way they help us dispel or absorb negative energies; jet, obsidian, black tourmaline and pink kunzite are good examples of this. Give these crystals an extra boost by dedicating them or charging them on a dark or waning moon cycle.

Dedicating for meditation or channelling: I very much like to dedicate stones such as lapis, amethyst, clear quartz or turquoise during dark moons when the energies are aligned for more introverted, inward-facing activities. I like to take these crystals into the darker parts of my garden or even into areas shaded slightly by rocks but still able to be graced by the sky. I try and retrieve them just before dawn to keep the integrity of the darkness intact.

SOLAR ENERGY

While I love to leave my crystals out basking in the silvery moonlight, there are some crystals that thrive under the fiery sun. I find that naturally gold or warm-coloured stones such as amber and citrine often need a good dose of solar energy to keep them happy, so don't be afraid to do so. When dedicating your crystals you will still need to cleanse them first in whichever manner works best for you, but here are some charging and dedication suggestions using solar energy that work for me.

Dedicating for health: leave out your crystals from dawn until dusk on three consecutive days that will be dedicated to health and healing. Midsummer is an ideal time to do this, as is the time around a new moon.

Dedicating for inspiration: get a boost from the biggest fire of all to fan your personal fires of inspiration: the sun. Place your stones on a natural surface such as grass or a plant and leave them out from dawn until dusk for seven days. Springtime is a great time to do this each year.

Gifts: when I am giving a crystal to a man I always leave it out under the sun for a day or so. The sun gives the stone a charging of masculine energy that I believe enables it to bind more quickly to its new owner. For women, leave your crystal under the moon instead.

THE MOON AND PLANTS

People all over the planet have been farming and gardening by the moon's cycles for millennia. The earth operates under a gravity field that is influenced by the moon (and also by other planets), which affects the growth of plants. Just as the moon influences the oceans and other bodies of water, it is believed the moon changes the level of water in the soil, affecting seedling and plant growth.

There are amazing farmer's almanacs you can buy for your region each year that give very detailed planting suggestions and harvesting recommendations, all guided by the moon and astrological information. (Check the Resources section at the end of the book for details.) This isn't a gardening diary but I have added some suggestions, and it certainly is worth mentioning the basic rules of thumb when it comes to gardening by the moon. As more and more of us choose to grow our own organic herbs, vegies and other plants, knowing how the moon may influence your patch could make the difference between a fair, good or bumper crop.

FULL MOON
As the water rises and swells within the soil it is a perfect time to plant seeds. It is also a good time to harvest some plants at the peak of their goodness.

WANING MOON
As the water level sinks it's time to plant below-ground plants such as potatoes, carrots, onions, parsnips and beetroot.

NEW MOON
Growth slows with the new moon, so this is the time to prune, trim, weed and fertilise. Apply any necessary natural pest control.

WAXING MOON
This is growth time again, as water begins to rise. It is a good time for planting above-ground crops such as pumpkin, tomatoes, cauliflower, kale, lettuce and spinach.

FERTILE ZODIAC SIGNS
Water and earth signs are considered the growth times for plants. When the moon enters these signs it's a fine time to plant or prune back for growth.

BARREN ZODIAC SIGNS
All your maintenance chores should be done when the moon is in fire and air signs.

JANUARY

◆ What would I like to create, experience and manifest this month?

_____

_____

_____

_____

◆ What are the important dates for me this month?

_____

_____

◆ What would give me joy this month?

_____

_____

◆ What am I devoted to?

_____

_____

◆ Ideas, musings, actions:

_____

_____

_____

DIANA

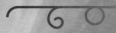

I find the beginning of the year the ideal time to take a breath and focus on what I want for the year. No doubt it will be different in some ways from last year, yet it is certainly worth spending time in being considered with my thinking and choosing some options. Choosing to work with a deity who excels in that kind of focus is always a good idea, so allow me to suggest the goddess Diana to start the year.

Diana is the Roman goddess of the moon, wild places, animals and the hunt. There would be few people who haven't come across a likeness of her as an athletic young woman in a short tunic, often surrounded by her hunting dogs and a stag and with a bow and arrows over her shoulder. As a child I found this image very compelling, and it is Diana's Greek counterpart (and very close in mythos) Artemis who is now my patroness.

Diana the lightbringer is a goddess of women for women. She sent her daughter Aradia to become flesh upon the earth as a maiden. Her feet bare, her body naked and moonstruck by the silver light of her mother in her lunar form, Aradia came to teach the word of her mother, that of the divine, to help those who were oppressed, tired and poor.

There isn't much to not like about Diana and Artemis as they embody female empowerment, a deep love for the wild earth and true focus. Focus is important if you are going to achieve anything important that you really want. If you have ever shot an arrow you understand the concentration, instinct, focus and control that is required for the action.

An archer will nock the arrow, judge the target, focus, breathe, focus, hold their breath and release the arrow by simply and steadily letting go. It is an apt process for life, really! Diana shows you that while you can ride the cycles of the moon you can also focus on what you want over time. You can bring your will to the situation along with your endurance.

Focus spell with Diana

THIS INVOCATION IS MUCH MORE EFFECTIVE IF YOU GO OUTSIDE INTO NATURE TO CAST IT. IF YOU CAN BE UNDER A FULL OR NEW MOON, ALL THE BETTER! CONSIDER IN ADVANCE WHERE YOU WANT MORE FOCUS WITHIN YOUR LIFE AND, IF YOU LIKE, GO FOR A RUN OR DO SOME MOVEMENT BEFORE THIS SPELL, WHICH WILL GET YOU INTO A WILDER STATE.

You'll need:

- a white or silver candle
- an arrowhead you have made or bought
- a small bowl of aqua luna (water left out under a full moon for blessing)
- incense

LIGHT THE CANDLE AND SAY: *'Lightbringer, lady of the wild, you who never miss, Diana of the hunt, I call your name and petition you for your support.'*

TAKE THE ARROWHEAD, DIP IT INTO THE AQUA LUNA AND SAY: *'I offer you a gift of this arrowhead in my devotion; may this be agreeable to you.*

'Great moon goddess, I ask you to help me focus and keep steady my gaze upon … [tell Diana where you wish to have her assist you, being as honest as you can be].

'I wish to not be diverted from my path. Help me not procrastinate or lose my interest. As you shoot and never miss, may this be so with what I aim for.'

LIGHT THE INCENSE AND SAY: *'I ask all this in your name.'*

Hold the arrowhead and pass it through the smoke, blessing it.

Blow out the candle then bury it in the garden or in a wild place.

27 Monday ☽

Waning

28 Tuesday ☽

Waning

29 Wednesday ☽

Waning

30 Thursday ☽

Waning

31 Friday ◗

Waning

New Year's Eve spell: set your intentions for 2022 if you haven't already done so. Do the spell with Jana and Janus of the gateway or mark the end of this year with a small ritual of gratitude before you go out to celebrate. Merely lighting a candle with intention and giving a special honouring of all the energies or deities that assisted you this year is a great start.

1 Saturday ●   January 2022

Dark Moon

Allow the moon of pure possibility to inspire you. Let go of what you don't need.

Welcome to a new year!

Catch the wave of global 'fresh start, new beginnings' energy. Release your intentions today!

2 Sunday ☽   new moon in Capricorn, 1.33 pm EST

This is the beginning of something powerful, so think big. Set intentions for resilience, stability and groundedness. Super new moon.

DECEMBER								**JANUARY**						
M	**T**	**W**	**T**	**F**	**S**	**S**		**M**	**T**	**W**	**T**	**F**	**S**	**S**
		1	2	3	4	5							**1**	**2**
6	7	8	9	10	11	12		3	4	5	6	7	8	9
13	14	15	16	17	18	19		10	11	12	13	14	15	16
20	21	22	23	24	25	26		17	18	19	20	21	22	23
27	**28**	**29**	**30**	**31**				24	25	26	27	28	29	30
								31						

3 Monday ◖

Waxing

4 Tuesday ◖

Waxing

5 Wednesday ◖

Waxing

6 Thursday ◖

Waxing

7 Friday

Waxing

Friday was named after Freyja, the Norse goddess of love, war and magic.

8 Saturday

Waxing

9 Sunday

Waxing

Nature hates a vacuum.

– THE GODDESS

JANUARY

M	T	W	T	F	S	S
					1	2
3	**4**	**5**	**6**	**7**	**8**	**9**
10	11	12	13	14	15	16
17	18	19	20	21	22	23
24	25	26	27	28	29	30
31						

JANUARY

10 Monday

Waxing

11 Tuesday

Waxing

12 Wednesday

Waxing

13 Thursday

Waxing

14 Friday ☽

Waxing

15 Saturday ☽

Waxing

16 Sunday ☽

Waxing

If you wish to grow your hair, this is a great time to trim it to promote growth.

JANUARY

M	T	W	T	F	S	S
					1	2
3	4	5	6	7	8	9
10	**11**	**12**	**13**	**14**	**15**	**16**
17	18	19	20	21	22	23
24	25	26	27	28	29	30
31						

17 Monday ○ full moon in Cancer, 6.48 pm, EST

Flow forward with fresh ideas and new processes for this year. Hope wins.

18 Tuesday

Waning

19 Wednesday ◑

Waning

20 Thursday ◑

Waning

21 Friday ◑

Waning

22 Saturday ◑

Waning

23 Sunday ◑

Waning

There are new beginnings within you every moment.

– THE GODDESS

JANUARY

M	T	W	T	F	S	S
				1	2	
3	4	5	6	7	8	9
10	11	12	13	14	15	16
17	**18**	**19**	**20**	**21**	**22**	**23**
24	25	26	27	28	29	30
31						

24 Monday 🌗

Waning

25 Tuesday 🌗

Waning

26 Wednesday 🌗

Waning

27 Thursday 🌗

Waning

28 Friday

Waning

29 Saturday

Waning

How are those new year's intentions going?

30 Sunday

Waning

JANUARY

M	T	W	T	F	S	S
					1	2
3	4	5	6	7	8	9
10	11	12	13	14	15	16
17	18	19	20	21	22	23
24	**25**	**26**	**27**	**28**	**29**	**30**
31						

FEBRUARY

◆ What would I like to create, experience and manifest this month?

_____

_____

_____

_____

◆ What are the important dates for me this month?

_____

_____

◆ What would give me joy this month?

_____

_____

◆ What am I devoted to?

_____

_____

◆ Ideas, musings, actions:

_____

_____

_____

APHRODITE

GODDESS OF THE MONTH: FEBRUARY

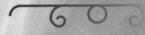

Love, love, love: it is the theme of poems, music, movies, books and paintings, yet it has to start with us! The most steady and powerful kind of love starts from the inside out; it does not rely on the opinions of what others think of you. It doesn't look for likes on social media, doesn't ask for compliments nor is it thirsty for external validation. Instead, it's radical self-love and Aphrodite is here to teach you.

While her role as a goddess for assisting with romantic love is well known, her primary lesson is one of self-love. Aphrodite shows you that you were born perfectly lovable and ready to accept your own beautiful self. She encourages the development of love from the inside out rather than from the outside in: in this way you do not rely on an external person to provide your sense of self-worth or self-esteem as you know, deep within yourself, who you are and that you are worth it. Without a healthy love of self you are reduced in personal power, often falling into petty jealousies, abuses of your body and numbing of your mind.

Aphrodite, beauty incarnate, was born of the sea foam, birthed out of a shell on a beach near the Greek island of Cythera. When she stepped upon the beach, flowers sprang from her footsteps. So lovely was this goddess that all of Olympus stopped to watch her. Eros in particular found a kindred spirit in Aphrodite, although her romantic charms were later enjoyed by Hermes, Poseidon and Dionysus. Her mythos is vast and she features in many stories from the fall of Troy to those of Eros and Psyche.

Call upon this famous goddess of love when you need more confidence and courage to build your love of self.

CONFIDENCE AND SELF-LOVE RITUAL

THIS SPELL SHOULD BE DONE AT THE TIME OF A NEW MOON.

You'll need:
- a silver candle
- a blue candle
- fragrant incense or rose oil
- a large shell
- some salted water (if you are not near the beach, water with a pinch of sea salt will do just fine) in a large bowl
- a small mirror

LIGHT THE BLUE CANDLE AND SAY: *'Aphrodite, born of foam, beauty and love incarnate: I ask you to support me today and bless me with your presence.'*

Light the incense or put a few drops of oil on the shell and place it in front of the blue candle.

SAY: *'Please accept my offering, gold-crowned queen of love.'*

WASH YOUR HANDS IN THE BOWL OF SALTED WATER AND SAY: *'I wash away all doubt. I wash away all that does not serve me. In your sea I wash away the lack of confidence I have for myself.'*

LIGHT THE SILVER CANDLE AND SAY: *'I wish to love myself fully from the inside out. Great queen, you teach me that a love of who I am extends outwards like a great ripple in the ocean, extending to others and to the world. This brings me confidence and joy.'*

Close your eyes and imagine the beautiful Aphrodite walking hand in hand along her island beach with you. Feel her love and the love within you grow.

Open your eyes and hold the mirror up to your face.

BREATHE DEEPLY AND LOOK AT YOUR IMAGE, THEN SAY: *'I see a goddess. I see my eyes with your blessing. Mirror back to me my worth, as I sometimes struggle to feel it.'*

REPEAT IN A SOFT CHANT: *'I am goddess, I am goddess, I am goddess.'*

Thank Aphrodite for her blessing and allow the candles to safely burn down. Throw the salted water down the drain without touching it.

WHEEL OF THE YEAR

Imbolc

1 FEBRUARY

Wake and shake! Just when you think spring is never going to come, one morning it all feels different: the bite is out of the wind; the temperature is just that little bit higher; the birds are out again and looking for a date; and the earth: you'd swear it was vibrating. And with that small sacred shake, the plants get all turned on and before you know it . . . *boom!* It's Imbolc.

The wheel has turned to 1 February and Imbolc, a celebration of the returning of the light after the depths of winter. It's the perfect time to ask for clarity of purpose, to set intentions for health and the body and to increase self-knowledge and allow your true light to shine.

Imbolc had its origins as a spring celebration honouring the Celtic goddess Brigid in her fire aspect. This beginning of the change of season was considered to be the time that Brigid's fire sparks again and awakens the earth. For me it always signals a time when I am able to shake off winter introversion and take more action towards what I want for the rest of the year. My work output increases, my movement patterns change and I choose to change what I eat to more seasonally spring foods. All in all, I begin to lighten up!

CELEBRATING IMBOLC

Brigid is the goddess of the wells and waters as well as fire, and any water left out for her to bless at this time has very special qualities. In the spirit of health, renewal and rebirth, it is said that if you wash your face in that water you will not age for another year, so what are you waiting for?

Leave outside a bowl with a small amount of fresh water in it on the night before Imbolc. Also, as a gift, leave out fresh cream, honey or milk or a small biscuit or cake. Brigid will bless your water along with any dew that has fallen, and you can use it the next morning.

Something very lovely and traditional to try is creating a Brigid's cross, a way of honouring the goddess and calling in good luck for your home. All you need is some straw or small flexible twigs from your garden. I hang the crosses as decorations on the trees in my garden and on my windowsills ready for Imbolc morning.

31 Monday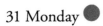

Dark moon.

Take a breather and relax. Allow the restful magic of the dark moon to do its work.

1 Tuesday, new moon in Aquarius, 12.46 am EST

Imbolc: the light is returning! May the blessings of Brigid be upon you. If you have collected it, use Brigid's Imbolc healing waters for your health and potions.

2 Wednesday

Waxing

3 Thursday

Waxing

4 Friday ◑

Waxing

5 Saturday ◑

Waxing

6 Sunday ◑

Waxing

Use your will, for it is yours.

– THE GODDESS

JANUARY								FEBRUARY						
M	T	W	T	F	S	S		M	T	W	T	F	S	S
				1	2			1	2	3	4	5	6
3	4	5	6	7	8	9		7	8	9	10	11	12	13
10	11	12	13	14	15	16		14	15	16	17	18	19	20
17	18	19	20	21	22	23		21	22	23	24	25	26	27
24	25	26	27	28	29	30		28						
31														

7 Monday ☽

Waxing

8 Tuesday ☽

Waxing

9 Wednesday ☽

Waxing

10 Thursday ☽

Waxing

11 Friday ☽

Waxing

12 Saturday ☽

Waxing

13 Sunday ☽

Waxing

FEBRUARY

M	T	W	T	F	S	S
	1	2	3	4	5	6
7	**8**	**9**	**10**	**11**	**12**	**13**
14	15	16	17	18	19	20
21	22	23	24	25	26	27
28						

14 Monday

Waxing

Happy Lupercalia (Valentine's Day)!

Forget Valentine's Day and get into the original celebration. The ancient Roman festival of Lupercalia celebrated virility, wildness, fertility and lust, so ride the energetic wave and cast a love spell to improve your current relationship or attract a new one that perfectly suits you.

15 Tuesday

Waxing

16 Wednesday, ◯ full moon in Leo, 11.56 am EST

Ask for what you want: clearly and openly.

17 Thursday

Waning

18 Friday 🌓

Waning

19 Saturday 🌓

Waning

20 Sunday 🌓

Waning

No one knows you better.

– THE GODDESS

FEBRUARY

M	T	W	T	F	S	S
	1	2	3	4	5	6
7	8	9	10	11	12	13
14	**15**	**16**	**17**	**18**	**19**	**20**
21	22	23	24	25	26	27
28						

21 Monday

Waning

22 Tuesday

Waning

23 Wednesday

Waning

24 Thursday

Waning

25 Friday 🌓

Waning

26 Saturday 🌓

Waning

27 Sunday 🌓

Waning

Don't be fooled by old talk. Listen to your cheer
squad, pom-poms and all.

– THE GODDESS

FEBRUARY

M	T	W	T	F	S	S
		1	2	3	4	5	6
7	8	9	10	11	12	13
14	15	16	17	18	19	20
21	**22**	**23**	**24**	**25**	**26**	**27**
28						

MARCH

- What would I like to create, experience and manifest this month?

_____

_____

_____

_____

- What are the important dates for me this month?

_____

_____

- What would give me joy this month?

_____

_____

_____

- What am I devoted to?

_____

_____

_____

- Ideas, musings, actions:

_____

_____

_____

NJÖRÐR

GOD OF THE MONTH: MARCH

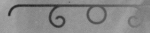

The year is well and truly in swing and it is always a wise move to have a deity of flow and prosperity on your side.

The Norse god Njörðr is perhaps not as well known as Thor or Odin or his daughter Freyja, but he was beloved by fishermen as he secured them a good catch and by the ancient Vikings as he ruled over the winds and flow of the seas. As a sea-faring and trading people this god meant wealth for the Vikings, and he was invoked for safety before a sea journey. Njörðr was prayed to for wealth as he could grant valuables, treasure and land to those he favoured.

As Njörðr originated from Vanaheimr and was not part of the tribe of Æsir he was different from Odin's family. Somewhat amusingly, it is known that he had beautiful feet. When the snow and mountain goddess Skaði was asked to choose a husband and could only see their feet to do so, she chose Njörðr. For a sea god of such power and force he was unusually benevolent and depicted as lacking in malice in poems. He was one of the few survivors of the end of the world cycle known as Ragnarök.

Call upon Njörðr when you require a boost to your finances or you need to build your wealth.

Flowful prosperity spell

BEFORE CASTING THIS SPELL CONSIDER SPECIFICALLY WHERE YOU NEED MORE MONEY OR PROSPERITY. THE SPELL IS BEST DONE ON AN INCOMING TIDE ON A WAXING PART OF THE MOON CYCLE. IT WOULD BE FANTASTIC IF IT COULD BE DONE ON A BEACH, BUT IF NOT YOUR GARDEN WILL BE FINE.

You'll need good-quality beer or mead or a salty lolly as an offering for Njörðr. I use shells, coins, beads or salt or anything that can be used as trade or currency.

SAY: *'I call your name, great god of the winds and seas, you who can grant wealth from hard work. Great Njörðr, assist me please.'*

HOLD UP THE BEER OR MEAD AND SAY:

'Hail to you, Njörðr, calmer of seas, winds and fire!'

Pour the beer on the waterline or on the ground in your garden, then tell Njörðr where you would like the boost to your prosperity.

COMPLETE THE SPELL WITH THIS INVOCATION:

'I humbly ask for your intercession. I humbly ask for your favour. Thank you for your consideration.'

Know your words will travel easily and quickly. Leave your offering for Njörðr and thank him. Take one action, no matter how small, toward your intention.

SPRING

BEING FRUITFUL

'Fecund' is a strange word but it certainly sums up spring. The word hails from the Latin word *fecundus*, meaning fruitful, but it means much more than that. Someone who demonstrates fecundity is someone who *is*: someone who demonstrates a high level of intellectual and physical productiveness, who births new ideas and concepts and who blossoms and grows.

Spring is the time you can flow forward as the wheel turns and dream and act in a way that enables you to shake off your cold coats and be more open and fecund. The slowness of winter, while wonderful for planning and rest, now gives way to the active nature of fiery spring.

Spring always proves to me that I will get a chance to try again, I will get a chance to grow, to change, to reach for something beyond what I have now. Spring gives me the opportunity to dream and to know that this dreaming can blossom into something real in time.

Like fall, spring is one of the shoulder seasons of transformation. It unwraps itself slowly but surely, which we catch sight of first in the returning of the light. Our day starts sooner, the birds begin singing earlier and for longer. The hard crust of the ground softens and small, hopeful, green shoots appear. Ice melts, as perhaps does your heart.

Many folk feel as though they want to open up their houses wide after being cocooned in winter. People begin to talk about decluttering and spring cleaning. Spring is also the perfect time for a 'spring clean' of old patterns and beliefs that you don't need to hold on to any more.

OSTARA FLOWER CROWN AND BLESSING

At any spring or Ostara celebration you will often see both men and women wearing flower crowns. The crowns can be complex or simple, with the symbology being that of a blossoming mind and spirit.

One of my favourite combinations of flowers and plants for a crown involves plants that have the medicine and meaning of love, fecundity, happiness, fresh starts and clear minds.

Combine the herbs of fresh mint, lemon balm, bay leaves and catmint. If you can use freshly harvested spring flowers from your garden; flowers of particular note would be cottage roses, daisies, dandelions, jasmine or lavender.

Create your crown around some wire circled to the circumference of your head, using florist's tape to attach the herbs and flowers. Once the crown has been created to your satisfaction it's time to bless it.

Take the crown outside and say:

'I hold a crown for my head that heralds all the joy of spring. I celebrate the season. I celebrate the goddesses of Ostara.

'I ask for a fresh start, new energy, a happy and sure blossoming of my mind, body and spirit.'

Put the crown on and say:

'I crown myself with a clear mind and fecundity.'

Ostara

Spring equinox, 20 March, 11.33 am EST

The wheel turns and we find ourselves at another time of balance, another equinox: Ostara. Ostara is the spring equinox, a time when we have perfect balance between the forces of dark and light, although from the morrow light will increase day by day. With this incremental return of light and warmth the earth energies increase greatly until their solar peak at Litha.

Ostara signals a time of celebration for expansion and the real signs of growth. It was traditionally celebrated as a time of planting, when people would tend their crops and ensure their farms ran well. Any unneeded extras that would get in the way of growth were removed. Old branches and dead plants were cleared and repairs from the damage of winter storms were carried out. This may translate in modern times as allowing what you no longer need to fall behind, as allowing the burdens of the past to slip away.

Ostara is the time to challenge yourself and grow: you can take that new risk, you can begin that new project, and you can lean towards hope and positivity.

CELEBRATING OSTARA

When you celebrate this festival keep a few key concepts in mind: growth, happiness and expansion. Really feel these three as actions, not just words.

When I am preparing my altar or doing workings for Ostara my first symbolic stop is always eggs, one of the most traditional symbols of Ostara (possibly from the myth of the bird and the Germanic goddess Eostre/Ostara). I have some lovely hand-painted wooden eggs I place on my altar, but also I use both boiled and fresh eggs in ritual. I paint them up and perform rituals with them. One of my favourites involves taking a fresh egg, decorating it carefully and then writing upon it words and images that represent new intentions and wishes for myself.

I crack the egg and bury it into the earth. I express thanks as I'm doing this for all I have and for all the expansion that will be. I then add some seeds to the piece of soil and water it.

As this is a key time for the earth to produce I will also often give thanks for everything the earth gives me. I'll do lots of spells and workings outside and honour the goddesses and gods of the green places such as Gaia, Artemis, Ceres, Cernunnos, Veres and the Green Man.

The other great thing to do for Ostara is to make a flower crown with all the fresh blossoms and herbs around. Make it as fragrant and as extravagant as you can, wear it and then hang it on your door or decorate your altar with it.

28 Monday

Waning

The last official day of winter.

1 Tuesday

Dark moon.

This is a great night to do shadow workings to heal yourself.

2 Wednesday, new moon in Pisces, 12.34 pm EST

The beautiful, gentle new moon will facilitate self-love and remove crippling doubt.

3 Thursday

Waxing

Thursday (Thor's Day) was named after the Norse god Thor.

4 Friday

Waxing

5 Saturday

Waxing

6 Sunday

Waxing

Observe the seasons – the bud, the fruit, the fall, the
compost – as all are as important as each other.

- THE GODDESS

FEBRUARY						
M	T	W	T	F	S	S
	1	2	3	4	5	6
7	8	9	10	11	12	13
14	15	16	17	18	19	20
21	22	23	24	25	26	27
28						

MARCH						
M	T	W	T	F	S	S
	1	2	3	4	5	6
7	8	9	10	11	12	13
14	15	16	17	18	19	20
21	22	23	24	25	26	27
28	29	30	31			

7 Monday

Waxing

8 Tuesday

Waxing

9 Wednesday

Waxing

10 Thursday

Waxing

11 Friday 🌓

Waxing

12 Saturday 🌓

Waxing

13 Sunday 🌓

Waxing

MARCH

M	T	W	T	F	S	S
	1	2	3	4	5	6
7	**8**	**9**	**10**	**11**	**12**	**13**
14	15	16	17	18	19	20
21	22	23	24	25	26	27
28	29	30	31			

14 Monday ◑

Waxing

15 Tuesday ◑

Waxing

How are your new year's intentions faring?

16 Wednesday ◑

Waxing

17 Thursday ◑

Waxing

18 Friday, ◯ full moon in Virgo, 3.17 am EDT

This is a moon to set intentions for excellence and focus. The work you do in the world is important.

19 Saturday ◗

Waning

20 Sunday , ◗ Ostara, spring equinox, 11.33 am EST

Waning

One of the most joyful festivals in the Wheel of the Year! The hours of night and day are equal, but from tomorrow the days will grow longer. Warmth and light are returning to the earth day by day; it is a beautiful time of joy and balance. Set intentions for health and life balance.

Awaken. Surge. Rest. Be still.

– THE GODDESS

MARCH

M	T	W	T	F	S	S
	1	2	3	4	5	6
7	8	9	10	11	12	13
14	**15**	**16**	**17**	**18**	**19**	**20**
21	22	23	24	25	26	27
28	29	30	31			

21 Monday ◑

Waning

22 Tuesday ◑

Waning

23 Wednesday ◑

Waning

Binding spells are at their most powerful in the waning cycle. What negative behaviour would you like to bind?

24 Thursday ◑

Waning

25 Friday

Waning

26 Saturday

Waning

27 Sunday

Waning

MARCH

M	T	W	T	F	S	S
		1	2	3	4	5	6
7	8	9	10	11	12	13
14	15	16	17	18	19	20
21	**22**	**23**	**24**	**25**	**26**	**27**
28	29	30	31			

APRIL

- What would I like to create, experience and manifest this month?

_____

_____

_____

_____

- What are the important dates for me this month?

_____

_____

- What would give me joy this month?

_____

_____

- What am I devoted to?

_____

_____

- Ideas, musings, actions:

_____

_____

_____

ANDROMACHE

Amazons are quite fashionable in popular culture, and particularly in movies. I for one am happy about that because women need role models with excellent leadership and physical skills.

Although it is certainly now more acceptable for women to be physically strong, they still tend to doubt their physical prowess and feel themselves to be weaker than men. Women often feel they are just not capable in this area, and studies show that men are more likely to overestimate their abilities in physical tasks and sports while women are more likely to underestimate their abilities. Sadly, the idea that a woman has to be smaller, weaker and quieter to be desired by men hauntingly persists. Healthy fierceness is a positive trait in situations that require it, and Andromache and her Amazonian sisters show us that boundaries are necessary for the success of the tribe.

Who was Andromache? Modern historians believe Andromache to be the queen Hippolyte, whose girdle Herakles had to obtain as part of his 12 labours. The very first depiction of this event is on ancient pottery that dates back to 700 BCE.

Andromache was the leader of the all-female warrior tribe of the Amazons, who were born on the backs of horses and rode as soon as they were able. No man lived within their tribe (as slaves only if at all), so in order to boost their numbers the women warriors would yearly invite neighbouring tribes of men to mate with them in a mass ritual. The resulting female babies were kept and raised as Amazons while the males were given to back to the men or left in exposure to die.

The women were trained in many forms of hand-to-hand combat but their most unique weapon was the labrys, a double-headed axe that was worn over the back and easily accessed while on horseback. Amazonian women were physically strong and matched any man in horsemanship and weapons skill. They were ferocious fighters, and it was considered to be an act of great courage and warrior craft to kill one. Ancient historian Herodotus said a young Amazon was only allowed to marry after killing a male in combat.

AMAZONIAN STRENGTH SPELL

When you need physical or mental strength, call upon the power of the Amazons and Andromache.

Gather together:

+ a drawing of a labrys (it doesn't have to be amazing!)
+ a small candle
+ incense (myrrh and frankincense are really nice)
+ fragrant body oil

PUT THE DRAWING NEAR THE CANDLE, THEN LIGHT BOTH IT AND THE INCENSE AND SAY:

'Queen of the Amazons, mighty Andromache: I call you for guidance. I call on you as part of the tribe of women, for your power and strength. Show me how to be strong! Bless me with your readiness and courage.'

Shut your eyes and imagine Andromache and her Amazons standing before you, powerful and unafraid and with their horses and weapons. Know they are strong intellectually and physically and in every way.

Visualise Andromache coming toward you and laying her hand upon your shoulder. Instantly feel her strength and power and the way that it pulses through you. Feel every cell in your body begin to electrically charge and rise and yourself becoming stronger, sharper, clearer.

Tell Andromache where you need strength and any other needs you have. Know that she is powerful and rewards those who strive and are courageous.

SAY: *'I am as strong as the Amazons. You are with me Andromache. I fear no ill.'*

Stay with the Amazons as long as you need to, then open your eyes and thank Andromache. Know you are stronger in every way. Massage the oil into your legs or arms and feel the muscles as you do so. Blow out the candle.

WHEEL OF THE YEAR

Beltaine (Bel Tan, Beltane)

30 April - 1 May

When I first started along the pagan and witchcraft path a number of decades ago I never saw anyone else like me doing ritual under a moon.

Wild and full of love magic, Beltaine demonstrates the intoxicating energy of life. It is the opposite on the Wheel of the Year to Samhain (Halloween), so where Samhain celebrates death and a void Beltaine is the embodiment of lusty life and super fertility.

Beltaine translates literally into the words 'good fire', and our ancestors took the returning of warmth and lifeblood to the land literally by lighting massive torches right through the country. Feasts and ceremonies accompanied the fires and it was a time of joy and happiness.

Some of the earliest Beltaine celebrations called for the May queen and king of the community to be united in ceremony. After ritual they would make love upon the earth to bring fertility to the soil. The community would also show their unity on their own land by wildly running, painting symbols upon their bodies, making music, drumming, telling stories and feasting.

The modern Beltaine is still seen in May Day celebrations in which there is dancing around a maypole. The pole is usually wrapped in red and white ribbons and has young maidens dancing around it. The origins of these dances are fertility based, honouring the forces that bring seeding and growth back to the soil.

Again, as at Samhain, the veils between the worlds are at their thinnest so it is also one of the two best nights of the year to perform divination. Imagine our ancient and not-so-ancient ancestors scrying by fire, tossing runes or doing Ogham wood readings.

If you are looking for the perfect energy to conceive a baby or an idea, here is your night!

CELEBRATING BELTAINE

I get up very early on Beltaine morning and light a candle. With this flame I ask for the season's blessings and that fertility and happiness be upon my house. I clear and clean my altar and decorate it in white and red, including big bunches of fresh flowers and ripe fruits. I also light candles. I then do some divination such as with oracle cards and do a reading to ask for answers to any questions I might have.

As the energy of Beltaine lends itself to potion making, it is on this day that I blend and make all kinds of healing salves and potions. I may also make some talismans for love, the healing of relationships and for conception and prosperity.

28 Monday

Waning

29 Tuesday

Waning

30 Wednesday

Waning

31 Thursday

Dark moon.

Relax and release and restore.

1 Friday, ☽ new moon in Aries, 2.24 am EDT

Stand aside your grudges and start afresh and clear.

2 Saturday ◑

Waxing

3 Sunday ◑

Waxing

MARCH								APRIL						
M	**T**	**W**	**T**	**F**	**S**	**S**		**M**	**T**	**W**	**T**	**F**	**S**	**S**
	1	2	3	4	5	6						1	2	3
7	8	9	10	11	12	13		4	5	6	7	8	9	10
14	15	16	17	18	19	20		11	12	13	14	15	16	17
21	22	23	24	25	26	27		18	19	20	21	22	23	24
28	**29**	**30**	**31**					25	26	27	28	29	30	

4 Monday ☽

Waxing

5 Tuesday ☽

Waxing

6 Wednesday ☽

Waxing

7 Thursday ☽

Waxing

8 Friday ☽

Waxing

9 Saturday ☽

Waxing

10 Sunday ☽

Waxing

APRIL

M	T	W	T	F	S	S
				1	2	3
4	**5**	**6**	**7**	**8**	**9**	**10**
11	12	13	14	15	16	17
18	19	20	21	22	23	24
25	26	27	28	29	30	

11 Monday

Waxing

12 Tuesday

Waxing

13 Wednesday

Waxing

14 Thursday

Waxing

15 Friday

Waxing

16 Saturday ○ full moon in Libra, 2.55 pm EDT

This is a powerful moon for setting intentions around positive health outcomes.

17 Sunday ◐

Waning

APRIL
M T W T F S S

				1	2	3
4	5	6	7	8	9	10
11	**12**	**13**	**14**	**15**	**16**	**17**
18	19	20	21	22	23	24
25	26	27	28	29	30	

18 Monday

Waning

19 Tuesday

Waning

20 Wednesday

Waning

21 Thursday

Waning

22 Friday

Waning

23 Saturday

Waning

24 Sunday

Waning

UN World Day for Laboratory Animals. Be conscious about products that have animal testing as part of their manufacture. You can choose cruelty free.

APRIL

M	T	W	T	F	S	S
				1	2	3
4	5	6	7	8	9	10
11	12	13	14	15	16	17
18	**19**	**20**	**21**	**22**	**23**	**24**
25	26	27	28	29	30	

25 Monday

Waning

26 Tuesday

Waning

27 Wednesday

Waning

28 Thursday

Waning

29 Friday ●

Dark moon

30 Saturday, ☽ new moon in Taurus, 4.28 pm EDT

This is a perfect moon for wishes around a new home or better environment.

Sow seeds for above-ground plants such as lettuce, cabbage and mint.

Happy Beltaine! Celebrate the good (bel) fire (tan). Delight in the most fertile of spring energies and growth today and tonight. Allow yourself a little wildness and make merry. This is a magical night for lovers and lovemaking. Decorate your altar with fresh flowers or make a maypole in your yard.

1 Sunday ◑

Waxing

APRIL							MAY						
M	T	W	T	F	S	S	M	T	W	T	F	S	S
				1	2	3							1
4	5	6	7	8	9	10	2	3	4	5	6	7	8
11	12	13	14	15	16	17	9	10	11	12	13	14	15
18	19	20	21	22	23	24	16	17	18	19	20	21	22
25	26	27	28	29	30		23	24	25	26	27	28	29
							30	31					

MAY

◆ What would I like to create, experience and manifest this month?

_____

_____

_____

_____

◆ What are the important dates for me this month?

_____

_____

◆ What would give me joy this month?

_____

_____

◆ What am I devoted to?

_____

_____

◆ Ideas, musings, actions:

_____

_____

_____

SARASVATI

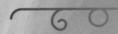

As we are still within spring, change and creation energy are strongly manifest and it is lovely to work with goddesses who embody this same kind of energy. The Hindu goddess Sarasvati, who exemplifies the arts, music and poets, is often pictured dressed all in white and sitting on the lotus of knowledge and light. She holds a biwa, a musical instrument that symbolises the importance of music and flowful knowledge. Hers is a delightfully airy, truly communicative energy, and she has an inspiring muse-like influence and helps you create something out of nothing.

Sarasvati is an important feminine force within the Hindu mythos. One of her aspects assists the triumvirate of Shiva, Vishnu and Brahma in the work of regenerating, creating the universe and all that is and keeping it balanced.

Her flowful nature is captured within her name, which comes from the words for 'pooling waters' and 'speech'. Her shrines are often near rivers or have water within them. The word *sara* also has within it the meaning of 'essence of self'; for any type of creative artist this would resonate strongly.

Music, painting, writing and oratory are within Sarasvati's domain, so those who engage in these arts would do well to respectfully engage her.

CREATIVITY RITUAL

THIS SPELL IS BEST CAST ON A NEW OR FULL MOON.

You will need:

* three small candles, each of a different colour
* some incense as a stick or resin or charcoal
* a talisman of creativity such as a crystal or piece of jewellery

Before casting the spell think about where you want more creativity:
in your work or art, some writing, a new project or a hobby?

LIGHT THE FIRST CANDLE AND SAY:

*'Beautiful goddess of delight, Sarasvati! Mother of eloquent speech
and melodious music, you who are wise and creative, I ask you to
assist me in the making of . . . [where you want creativity].'*

LIGHT THE SECOND CANDLE AND SAY:

*'Sarasvati, goddess of creativity, you who are music and you
who forms art, grant me the gift of flowful creation.'*

LIGHT THE INCENSE AND THE FINAL CANDLE AND SAY:

'Sarasvati, allow my creations to be and give pleasure.'

PASS THE TALISMAN THROUGH THE SMOKE OF THE INCENSE AND SAY:

'I now create a talisman of creativity in your name. Thank you.'

Allow the candles to burn down safely. Begin your project,
keeping the talisman with you or in your working area.

2 Monday ◑

Waxing

3 Tuesday ◑

Waxing

Tuesday was named after Twia, the Celtic/Germanic god of war and the sky. The Norse god Tyr is also closely identified with this day.

4 Wednesday ◑

Waxing

5 Thursday ◑

Waxing

6 Friday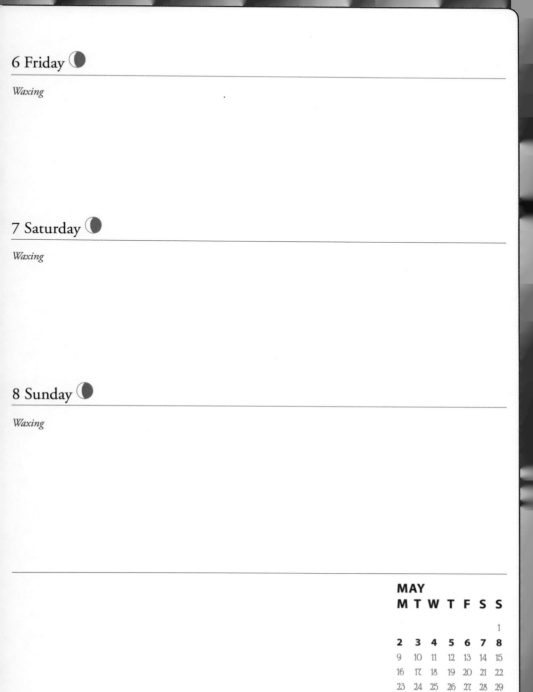

Waxing

.

7 Saturday

Waxing

8 Sunday

Waxing

MAY

M	T	W	T	F	S	S
						1
2	3	4	5	6	7	8
9	10	11	12	13	14	15
16	17	18	19	20	21	22
23	24	25	26	27	28	29
30	31					

9 Monday

Waxing

10 Tuesday

Waxing

11 Wednesday

Waxing

12 Thursday

Waxing

13 Friday

Waxing

14 Saturday

Waxing

15 Sunday

Waxing

MAY

M	T	W	T	F	S	S
						1
2	3	4	5	6	7	8
9	**10**	**11**	**12**	**13**	**14**	**15**
16	17	18	19	20	21	22
23	24	25	26	27	28	29
30	31					

16 Monday, ○ full moon in Scorpio, 12.14 am EDT

A wonderful moon to cast protective spells and enliven talismans of success and confidence.

17 Tuesday ◗

Waning

18 Wednesday ◗

Waning

19 Thursday ◗

Waning

20 Friday

Waning

21 Saturday

Waning

22 Sunday

Waning

MAY

M	T	W	T	F	S	S
						1
2	3	4	5	6	7	8
9	10	11	12	13	14	15
16	**17**	**18**	**19**	**20**	**21**	**22**
23	24	25	26	27	28	29
30	31					

23 Monday 🌗

Waning

24 Tuesday 🌗

Waning

25 Wednesday 🌗

Waning

26 Thursday 🌗

Waning

27 Friday

Waning

28 Saturday

Waning

29 Sunday

Dark moon.

Plan a gentle and restorative night in for yourself.

MAY
M T W T F S S

						1
2	3	4	5	6	7	8
9	10	11	12	13	14	15
16	17	18	19	20	21	22
23	**24**	**25**	**26**	**27**	**28**	**29**
30	31					

JUNE

- What would I like to create, experience and manifest this month?

_____

_____

_____

_____

- What are the important dates for me this month?

_____

_____

- What would give me joy this month?

_____

_____

- What am I devoted to?

_____

_____

- Ideas, musings, actions:

_____

_____

_____

HEPHAESTUS

GOD OF THE MONTH: JUNE

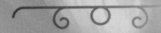

Perfectly imperfect, what the Greek god Hephaestus lacked in beauty he certainly made up for in intelligence, ingenuity and inventiveness. There was nothing that Hephaestus (or Vulcan in his Roman embodiment) could not make, an incredible talent that made him both feared and respected among other deities, although as he was not as perfectly formed as the other beauteous gods he was made to feel different and lesser than them.

In the Roman legend Hephaestus' mother Juno tried to throw him off a cliff and bury him in a volcano. The Greek legend tells of his mother Hera flinging him from Olympus down to the island of Lemnos when she saw what she had borne. On Lemnos, Thetis (the mother of Achilles) raised Hephaestus and he invented blacksmithing, the art of the forge.

Hephaestus' creativity and inventiveness abounded and he produced objects that were both practical and magical. The winged boots of Hermes were made by his hand, along with the silver armour of Achilles, Helio's sun chariot, the unbreakable chains that held poor Prometheus to his rock and incredibly the first woman, Pandora, was also his divine handiwork.

Hephaestus never quite forgave his mother for her slight upon him, and he made Hera a golden throne untouched in its artistry under the guise of a gift. As soon as Hera sat upon the throne mechanical coils sprang forth that trapped her in the chair; no matter how hard she tried she could not free herself. The son she so looked down upon now had the upper hand, and he negotiated his return into the realm of the gods with Venus (Aphrodite) as his wife.

When you need to think outside the box or come up with a new solution or big idea, Hephaestus is your god.

INVENTIVENESS RITUAL

Being different and thinking differently is the stuff of genius, but it can be hard when people wish us to be just like them. However, we could all benefit from a bit more inventiveness and authenticity in our lives and within our communities. This spell can be done on any moon cycle. You will need a hammer and a piece of metal to bang on: anything you don't mind denting a little! It should make a good ringing sound when you strike it if that is possible.

LIGHT A RED CANDLE AND RHYTHMICALLY HIT THE HAMMER ON THE METAL JUST AS A BLACKSMITH WOULD. SING OR SAY:

'Let's sing the praises of Hephaestus
Let's hear his hammer beat
Let's sing the praises of Hephaestus
Feel his mastery and feel his heat.

'Let me learn what I can from Hephaestus
Thinking different is the way
I learn what I can from Hephaestus
More authentic day by day.

'Let's create what I can from Hephaestus
More ingenuity in every beat
Let's create what I have from Hephaestus
A genius solution is complete!'

BANG HARD THREE TIMES ON THE METAL AND REPEAT:

'I forge my way.'

Shut your eyes and ask Hephaestus to give you some hint or first step to the solution to your problem, project or invention. Write anything and everything that comes to mind down and then act on anything that seems urgent.

Leave the metal piece on your altar or throw it in a fire to complete the invocation.

SUMMER

If winter is a more introverted season, summer is the big, bright, loud and proud opposite. The energy is big: growth is at its peak and there are long, luxurious days, warm nights and a great deal of social life.

Summer energy is wonderful not only to get out and about, but it is also deeply satisfying for magic. When you plug in to earth at summertime there is a buzz about it: you can have your feet in the highly vibrating soil and feel the life-giving sensation of sunshine. You need sunshine to produce vital vitamin D and light to balance your circadian rhythm; it's not just plants that are solar powered!

My garden grows exponentially at this time of year, the sweet flowers of spring giving way to the fruiting of the passionfruit vine and the explosion of tropical flowers such as frangipani. The bird wars of spring have phased into young birds being fledged and taught the ways of feathered life, and often local magpies and wattlebirds bring their large teens for a look. Some birds such as the local brush turkeys have been working their mounds for many months, and finally the little babies dig their way out of the eggs and curate piles of leaves and sticks so they can hide from predators.

The downsides to all of this joy – depending on where you live – are drought and excess heat. Australia is the driest continent after Antarctica, so extremes of heat and years of drought and fires are common. There is a need for us to turn our collective attention to combating this before it is too late.

There has always been a certain sensuality to summer: we show more flesh and experience the sun on our skin, and summer storms bring big fat drops to fall upon our hair to relieve us in the evening. We eat outside; we stop to place flowers in our hair and lift our noses to take in the night breezes; we play in the ocean or rivers; we listen to different music. We feel and act more alive.

MIDSUMMER MAGIC AND MISCHIEF

When I was young my grandmother, who was of Irish descent, warned me about the fae on midsummer's eve. She wasn't a love 'n' light person who thought the fae were all sparkles and pretty wings; she believed the real fae were a bit more crafty and you had to respect them and be aware of their mischievous natures.

Our ancient ancestors who travelled to the solstice festivals of Litha would have been on the road the night before, so they would usually sleep outdoors under the stars. They were warned to pay particular attention on the journey to where they were going because the fae were very active on this night and could sweep a person away and leave them with no money or sense. Thus you could disappear off with the faeries!

According to my gran the way to not end up bleeding at the bottom of your garden not knowing where you were was to make sure you were always kind and respectful to the fae, but particularly so on this night. She showed me how to prepare little presents for them and to involve them in our midsummer's eve celebrations. You can involve your children in the many ways to do this, as they love trying to sight the good folk in the garden.

I collect beautiful little plates and tiny saucers with lots of patterns and add strawberries, sweets and cream and a bit of fresh honey from my hives. I sometimes add a tiny note telling them I'm glad they are there and how happy I am that they share the garden.

I place the gifts wherever I think the fae might see them or near places they might be. If you really look around you'll find small worlds in your garden or local park that have a 'feel' to them if you are sensitive enough to notice. They may be places where moss and mushrooms spring up or where dandelions grow, holes in a tree trunk or where it smells fresh with flowers.

When you create gifts for the fae and spend time out on this amazing night you'll feel your own magic and happiness rising. You may feel light and happy and perhaps a little mischievous. Allow this good magical energy to flow through you and take a little for yourself.

Litha

SUMMER SOLSTICE, 21 JUNE, 5.13 AM EDT

The wheel turns again and it is the big energy of Litha we have to play with now. Litha is a powerful solstice (sun) festival and we get to experience the longest day of the year and the shortest night.

The solstice was marked carefully by many of our ancestors to capture the peak earth energies – peak sun, warmth and daylight are alchemic, after all – and because, once this day is gone, the light slowly recedes and the hours of night grow longer, meaning less time, warmth and light to grow food. Soon the colder months would arrive, so Litha was a reminder that the sunny, warm times would not be around forever and preparations must begin for the next season.

What does Litha offer you if you do not get your food from your garden? Litha reminds you to charge up the energy of your body and ensure you are treating it well and that it glows with vitality. Talismans and workings for health and vitality are perfect for Litha. Free yourself from your bad habits and allow your body and mind to be light, illuminated and powerful. Sound good?

Litha is a reminder of the fullness of all kinds of prosperity: money and career, certainly, but also the pleasure of a rich and varied life, the richness of friends and laughter, the wealth of a peaceful mind and strong spirit. If you don't already have these things you can set intentions for them now, and if you do have them you can do workings for gratitude and reciprocity.

CELEBRATING LITHA

Litha rituals are really easy to do because just standing in the sunshine for a couple of minutes and soaking it all up will get you in the swing of things!

For those who want to do more there is plenty to try. I get up just before dawn because I want to see the sun rise and feel the first rays of the longest day of the year. I light a candle to respect Litha's fire element and dress in something flame or golden coloured. I go into my garden or to the beach and place my feet upon the earth, plugging in and pulling up. Breath by breath I allow that feeling to expand mightily and flood my body with Litha energy, which is big and bold so there is plenty of it. I take some within myself and also ripple it out to the world. To be able to channel such energy and then share it on a day such as this is a wondrous thing to offer to the world.

Litha traditionally celebrates the masculine divine. Solar energy is considered to be a masculine energy, so I make offerings or devotions to all the gods I work with.

30 Monday, ☽ new moon in Gemini, 7.30 am EDT

This is the second new moon of the month, so make it count. Set intentions for the birth or start of something you have always wanted.

31 Tuesday

Waxing

1 Wednesday

Waxing

2 Thursday

Waxing

3 Friday 🌓

Waxing

4 Saturday 🌓

Waxing

5 Sunday 🌓

Waxing

You are the magic.

- THE GODDESS

| MAY | | | | | | | JUNE | | | | | | |
M	T	W	T	F	S	S	M	T	W	T	F	S	S
						1			1	2	3	4	5
2	3	4	5	6	7	8	6	7	8	9	10	11	12
9	10	11	12	13	14	15	13	14	15	16	17	18	19
16	17	18	19	20	21	22	20	21	22	23	24	25	26
23	24	25	26	27	28	29	27	28	29	30			
30	31												

6 Monday

Waxing

7 Tuesday

Waxing

8 Wednesday

Waxing

9 Thursday

Waxing

10 Friday ◑

Waxing

11 Saturday ◑

Waxing

12 Sunday ◑

Waxing

Be still. Soften.

– THE GODDESS

JUNE

M	T	W	T	F	S	S
		1	2	3	4	5
6	**7**	**8**	**9**	**10**	**11**	**12**
13	14	15	16	17	18	19
20	21	22	23	24	25	26
27	28	29	30			

13 Monday ◐

Waxing

14 Tuesday, ○ full moon in Sagittarius, 7.51 am EDT

Super full moon

A gregarious and social full moon that is excellent for setting intentions for positive and long-lasting relationships of all kinds.

15 Wednesday ◑

Waning

16 Thursday ◑

Waning

17 Friday ☽

Waning

18 Saturday ☽

Waning

19 Sunday ☽

Waning

Rest indeed in the warmth of the dark for there is plenty to see if we allow it.

– THE GODDESS

JUNE

M	T	W	T	F	S	S
		1	2	3	4	5
6	7	8	9	10	11	12
13	**14**	**15**	**16**	**17**	**18**	**19**
20	21	22	23	24	25	26
27	28	29	30			

20 Monday ◑

Waning

It's midsummer's eve, one of the most magical nights of the whole year. The mischievous fae in your garden and wild places should be honoured on this evening! It is a great night for divination and for having fun with your children. Traditional gifts of strawberries, honey and milk are left out in wild places for the local fae. I add glitter and shiny objects to really attract the fae.

21 Tuesday, ◑ Litha, summer solstice, 5.13 am EDT

Waning

This is the day to honour the masculine divine in all its forms and celebrate the year's biggest festival of the sun. Arise early at dawn, light a candle and catch as much energy as you can; it's the longest day of the year, after all!

22 Wednesday ◑

Waning

23 Thursday ◑

Waning

24 Friday ◐

Waning

25 Saturday ◐

Waning

26 Sunday ◐

Waning

This is a good day to trim your hair if you want it to keep it in a similar style.

A flame burns only if it is fed.

– THE GODDESS

JUNE

M	T	W	T	F	S	S
		1	2	3	4	5
6	7	8	9	10	11	12
13	14	15	16	17	18	19
20	**21**	**22**	**23**	**24**	**25**	**26**
27	28	29	30			

27 Monday ●

Dark moon.

Enjoy this restful and introspective moon.

28 Tuesday, ☽ new moon in Cancer, 10.52 pm EDT

Micro new moon

This is an effective moon for working with balancing emotions and for peace and calm.

29 Wednesday ◐

Waxing

30 Thursday ◐

Waxing

1 Friday ☽

Waxing

2 Saturday ☽

Waxing

Saturday was named after the Roman god Saturn.

3 Sunday ☽

Waxing

JUNE								JULY							
M	**T**	**W**	**T**	**F**	**S**	**S**		**M**	**T**	**W**	**T**	**F**	**S**	**S**	
		1	2	3	4	5						**1**	**2**	**3**	
6	7	8	9	10	11	12		4	5	6	7	8	9	10	
13	14	15	16	17	18	19		11	12	13	14	15	16	17	
20	21	22	23	24	25	26		18	19	20	21	22	23	24	
27	**28**	**29**	**30**					25	26	27	28	29	30	31	

JULY

♦ What would I like to create, experience and manifest this month?

_____

_____

_____

_____

♦ What are the important dates for me this month?

_____

_____

♦ What would give me joy this month?

_____

_____

♦ What am I devoted to?

_____

_____

♦ Ideas, musings, actions:

_____

_____

_____

AGNI

GOD OF THE MONTH: JULY

In many cultures fire is the first element, that which creates all else. Fire is the driver, the creator and, sometimes, the destroyer. It keeps us warm and our food cooked, and the hearth is considered to be the heart of a home.

Fire, the element of summer, represents passion and spawns the physical motivation to get things done. It is a creative element that is easily coupled with the air element that feeds it. Many elemental systems introduced the idea that the universe was made from a primordial fire that generated the four elements, an idea that still exists in the idea that the soul is situated around the heart and that passion and love are warm and heartfelt.

Fire is important within the tenets of Hinduism: marrying couples walk around fire to signify their commitment and vows, and the cooking hearth in each home represents the family and gives the fire that cooks food for nourishment. Agni is the Hindu god of fire and is its embodiment; his energy is the source and essence of all fire in the world. He is the god of lightning and the spark that begins every fire, and the god of all sacrificial and sacred flames. Agni rules over anything flammable such as incense, resin or matches. As sacrifices are offered in fires, statues of Agni's likeness may be found where the fire element lives: in the south-east corner of temples.

Agni appears often with black or very dark skin. He has four arms and sometimes two heads (representing both hearth and sacrificial fires), and he either rides a goat or has a chariot with four red horses and seven wheels (representing the seven winds). Agni can be called upon when you need more passion and fire in your life. He can also be petitioned if you have too much fire and to control heated emotions like anger.

SUMMER FIRE MEDITATION

I LIKE TO DO THIS MEDITATION ON A WARM SUMMER DAY. IT IS ESPECIALLY USEFUL WHEN YOU FEEL A BIT STUCK OR INFLEXIBLE. WEAR SOMETHING RED OR ORANGE IF YOU LIKE.

Breathe deeply. Centre. Connect your bones or feet with the earth. Breathe again.

Light some incense and a candle. Take a deep breath and focus on the candle flame, allowing your eyes to relax and softly observe the dancing flame.

SAY: *'I call upon you, Agni, the embodiment of all fire. Allow me to feel the warmth of passion within me. Allow me to feel the electricity of your heat, allow it to enliven my whole body and soul.*

I call upon the spark of life, the lightning of the sky, the sweet burning of resin: they are all powerful for my mind, body and spirit. Inspire me and allow every cell to dance with vitality.'

Shut your eyes and imagine every single cell in your body lighting up with a small warm flame or a charge of gentle electricity. Visualise a flow of vital power warming every cell, cleansing and balancing them. Imagine your whole body glowing in power and delight. Stay in this feeling for as long as you like.

WHEN YOU ARE READY OPEN YOUR EYES, CLAP SEVEN TIMES AND SAY: *'I thank you for your blessings of power and passion, great god Agni.'*

Allow the candle flame to safely burn down.

4 Monday

Waxing

5 Tuesday

Waxing

6 Wednesday

Waxing

7 Thursday

Waxing

8 Friday

Waxing

9 Saturday

Waxing

10 Sunday

Waxing

Flowers don't fly to bees.

Develop stillness.

– THE GODDESS

JULY

M	T	W	T	F	S	S
				1	2	3
4	**5**	**6**	**7**	**8**	**9**	**10**
11	12	13	14	15	16	17
18	19	20	21	22	23	24
25	26	27	28	29	30	31

11 Monday ☽

Waxing

12 Tuesday ☽

Waxing

13 Wednesday, ○ full moon in Capricorn, 2.37 pm EDT

Get it done! Get organised with your intentions: plan and take action.

Super full moon.

14 Thursday ☾

Waning

15 Friday ◐

Waning

16 Saturday ◐

Waning

17 Sunday ◐

Waning

Be as the river stone surrounded by a raging river.

– THE GODDESS

JULY

M	T	W	T	F	S	S
				1	2	3
4	5	6	7	8	9	10
11	**12**	**13**	**14**	**15**	**16**	**17**
18	19	20	21	22	23	24
25	26	27	28	29	30	31

18 Monday ☽

Waning

19 Tuesday ☽

Waning

20 Wednesday ☽

Waning

21 Thursday ☽

Waning

22 Friday

Waning

23 Saturday

Waning

24 Sunday

Waning

We sometimes think the darkness is forever.

But no: nothing is forever.

– THE GODDESS

JULY

M	T	W	T	F	S	S
				1	2	3
4	5	6	7	8	9	10
11	12	13	14	15	16	17
18	**19**	**20**	**21**	**22**	**23**	**24**
25	26	27	28	29	30	31

25 Monday ◑

Waning

Harvest below-ground vegetables this week.

26 Tuesday ◑

Waning

27 Wednesday ●

Dark moon.

This is a perfect night to do some shadow work and rid yourself of a bad habit or old outdated belief.

28 Thursday, ☽ new moon in Leo, 1.54 pm EDT

Blow your own trumpet! Start something authentic that is uniquely yours.

29 Friday

Waxing

30 Saturday

Waxing

31 Sunday

Waxing

The light always returns.

– THE GODDESS

JULY

M	T	W	T	F	S	S
				1	2	3
4	5	6	7	8	9	10
11	12	13	14	15	16	17
18	19	20	21	22	23	24
25	**26**	**27**	**28**	**29**	**30**	**31**

AUGUST

- What would I like to create, experience and manifest this month?

_____

_____

_____

_____

- What are the important dates for me this month?

_____

_____

- What would give me joy this month?

_____

_____

- What am I devoted to?

_____

_____

- Ideas, musings, actions:

_____

_____

_____

EUROPA

The mythos of Europa is strange and contentious, but her lasting legacy is that the continent of Europe was named after her.

It was said Europa was a beautiful Phoenician princess who was light and fair of face. She had a dream one night about two women who were fighting over her, and she understood that they were not actually women but were continents of the earth. One, 'Asia', said that since Europa was Phoenician she belonged to her, but the other one, who had no name, said that Europa's past was no longer important and that a mighty god would give her a new land.

The next day, a beautiful one, Europa and her ladies decided to go out and have a picnic by the sea. They were eating and making flower crowns, enjoying the sunshine. Europa was unaware that Zeus had seen her and wanted her for his own. He knew that Europa was a shy and inexperienced young woman who would no doubt rebuff him, so he turned himself into a glorious white bull.

The white bull wandered over to the women, and such was its unusual glowing beauty that the women were not afraid and approached it. Zeus as the bull was gentle and affectionate, and the women covered him in floral garlands and fed and played with him. The bull lowered himself and offered his back to Europa, who was enchanted and began to ride him. Zeus got closer and closer to the waves of the sea and was soon swimming over the foam with Europa on his back, leaving the other women on the beach.

The bull continued to swim, surrounded by sea nymphs and dolphins. Europa realised this was no ordinary bull, and Zeus explained who he was. They travelled to the island of Crete, where Europa became a queen and bore Zeus famous sons such as Minos and Rhadamanthus.

Over time Europa's mythos and worship became more connected to the moon cycles and the growing of food (nourishment). Symbols of the cornucopia began to be made in art renditions of her.

HEALTH AND NOURISHMENT SPELL

THIS IS A WONDERFUL SPELL FOR PERSONAL GOOD HEALTH AND FOR RECOVERY IF YOU HAVE BEEN ILL. IF YOU HAVE REGULAR ISSUES WITH FOOD OR DIGESTION IN ANY WAY THIS SPELL MAY ASSIST YOU. IT IS BEST CAST UNDER A NEW OR FULL MOON.

On your altar or wherever you are casting gather together a cornucopia of seasonal foods and herbs, making it as attractive as you can.

You'll need:

◆ a green candle
◆ a small bowl of aqua luna (water left out under a full moon)
◆ an offering of grain (any grain is fine: wheat, polenta, lentils or rice)

LIGHT THE CANDLE AND SAY: *'Beautiful Europa, fair of face, broad and bright as the moon, I come before you today to ask you for your blessings and protection upon me.'*

FLICK SOME OF THE AQUA LUNA OVER THE CORNUCOPIA AS A BLESSING AND SAY:

'I ask that I am nourished in all ways, that I have balance and healing in my body and that . . . [state here anything extra with regard to food and healing].'

PLACE THE GRAIN ON OUR ALTAR OR ON THE GROUND AND SAY: *'I offer this grain in your name.'*

TAKE A SIP OF THE AQUA LUNA AND SAY: *'Queen Europa, beloved mother, I humbly ask that all will be as I have asked.'*

Thank Europa. Leave the grain as an offering; do not eat it or the food in the cornucopia yourself. This should be given to the earth or an animal or composted.

Take at least one step towards your goal.

WHEEL OF THE YEAR

Lammas

1 August

Feeling real gratitude for what you have is something you should consider doing on a regular basis. It shouldn't be a comparison between yourself and others but rather an examination of what the harvest of your own life is. Really seeing what you have and how far you have come, and understanding how you have journeyed from one year to another and what you should be grateful for is very powerful.

In the lives of farming peoples a couple of thousand years ago harvest time was a big deal. If you have ever grown your own vegetables or even a few pots of herbs you'll know how grateful and happy you feel when you're ready to harvest and eat the food you have grown with your own hands, so imagine what whole communities that had worked hard to produce food over the seasons had to be happy about.

Getting together to assist each other with harvesting and the trade that surrounded these activities was a grand excuse for villagers to get together and celebrate the bounty. It was also a time to share news and gossip and to perhaps arrange a marriage or see extended family.

HOW TO CELEBRATE LAMMAS

The smell of freshly baked bread is what I associate with Lammas; I always start by baking. I normally try and prepare the dough and let it rise the night before, then bake it on Lammas morning. It really doesn't matter how badly it turns out: it always smells good!

I decorate my altar with food that represents the harvest; it could be lots of produce from my garden that I'm growing, but traditionally it is fruits such as apples and pears or seeds and vegetables. The Lammas altar colours are gold, orange, brown and dark green.

I may invite others over for a feast and have everyone bring a plate. Very popular, of course, are baked goods, so we always have many cakes. Someone brings home-made mead and someone else makes candles and brings them to decorate the table. As the candles are lit everyone is invited to share about what they are grateful for and what their personal harvest is for this time.

If you have experienced an uncertain year, taking the time to celebrate or at least mark what you have achieved is important for your confidence and mental health. Feeling as though you are progressing and changing for the better brings peace and relief. Knowing that others support you and see you and what you are trying to achieve can make all the difference.

1 Monday ◑

Waxing

Lammas: the traditional time for first harvest and a time of gratitude. Express your gratitude for the harvest of your life so far.

2 Tuesday ◑

Waxing

3 Wednesday ◑

Waxing

4 Thursday ◑

Waxing

5 Friday

Waxing

6 Saturday

Waxing

7 Sunday

Waxing

Plug in. Feel the earth stirring.

– THE GODDESS

AUGUST

M	T	W	T	F	S	S
1	**2**	**3**	**4**	**5**	**6**	**7**
8	9	10	11	12	13	14
15	16	17	18	19	20	21
22	23	24	25	26	27	28
29	30	31				

8 Monday 🌓

Waxing

9 Tuesday 🌓

Waxing

10 Wednesday 🌓

Waxing

11 Thursday, ○ full moon in Aquarius, 9.35 pm EDT

This is an expansive moon when you can turn big dreams into reality. Don't just think about you: think about the bigger picture for all.

12 Friday ☽

Waning

13 Saturday ☽

Waning

14 Sunday ☽

Waning

Cracking open what is frozen and rigid.

– THE GODDESS

AUGUST

M	T	W	T	F	S	S
1	2	3	4	5	6	7
8	**9**	**10**	**11**	**12**	**13**	**14**
15	16	17	18	19	20	21
22	23	24	25	26	27	28
29	30	31				

15 Monday 🌖

Waning

16 Tuesday 🌖

Waning

17 Wednesday 🌗

Waning

18 Thursday 🌗

Waning

19 Friday ◑

Waning

20 Saturday ◑

Waning

21 Sunday ◑

Waning

The blood rush of change can be felt with every heart beat.

– THE GODDESS

AUGUST

M	T	W	T	F	S	S
1	2	3	4	5	6	7
8	9	10	11	12	13	14
15	**16**	**17**	**18**	**19**	**20**	**21**
22	23	24	25	26	27	28
29	30	31				

22 Monday ◐

Waning

23 Tuesday ◐

Waning

24 Wednesday ◐

Waning

25 Thursday ◐

Waning

26 Friday

Dark moon.

Joyfully let go. There is nothing negative to keep here.

27 Saturday, new moon in Virgo, 4.17 am EDT

Set intentions for wisdom and greater discernment.

28 Sunday

Waxing

The warmth and light are returning with reducing fall: it's time to make some changes! Simplify? A seasonal diet change?

AUGUST

M	T	W	T	F	S	S
1	2	3	4	5	6	7
8	9	10	11	12	13	14
15	16	17	18	19	20	21
22	**23**	**24**	**25**	**26**	**27**	**28**
29	30	31				

SEPTEMBER

◆ What would I like to create, experience and manifest this month?

_____

_____

_____

_____

◆ What are the important dates for me this month?

_____

_____

◆ What would give me joy this month?

_____

_____

◆ What am I devoted to?

_____

_____

◆ Ideas, musings, actions:

_____

_____

_____

KĀNE

GOD OF THE MONTH: SEPTEMBER

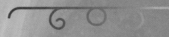

Kāne is the god of light, creation and the sky and is one of the most important gods of the Hawaiian nation along with Lono, Kanaloa and Kū. Kāne is widely worshipped and is considered to have had a key role in creating humans. The Hawaiian/Polynesian view of creation begins with Po, a void but also a place of dark chaos without borders similar to the ancient Greek Khaos, a place of everything and nothing that resonates with the idea of the big bang.

Just like the Greek mythos that Eros (love) began to organise itself from Khaos, Kāne became aware of his existence and consciousness and breathed and wrenched himself by a powerful act of sheer will away from Po. Lono and Kū became aware of themselves and of Kāne and also pulled themselves free of the void. Kāne concentrated hard and filled his being with light that illuminated the darkness of Po and lessened its power. Kū concentrated and brought solid substance to the new universe, while Lono focused and brought the vibration of sound across and through the universe.

The three gods wished to create more so they brought all the other deities and spirits into existence. They gathered clay from the four corners of the earth, mixed it with their own spit and formed it into the shape of a man without a head. Kāne took a magical white clay and formed it into the head of the man, then the clay man was enlivened by the breath of God. The first man was created in the image of Kāne. Hāloa, the breath of life of Kāne, lives on in Hawaiian and Polynesian cultures through greetings and healing practices.

When you wish to weave the powers of manifestation Kāne is a fantastic ally, but do note that while this god requires no complex or fancy prayer he does expect good and rightful action: it isn't what you say but what you do that counts.

Manifestation invocation to Kāne

IT IS BEST TO CAST THIS SPELL AT THE TIME OF A FULL MOON. ENSURE YOU KNOW WHERE THE FOUR DIRECTIONS ARE FROM WHERE YOU STAND (MOST MOBILE PHONES HAVE A COMPASS WITHIN THEM SO THIS SHOULD BE EASY TO DO). BEFORE CASTING THE SPELL, THINK ABOUT WHAT YOU WISH TO MANIFEST.

Get a glass or flask of water and place a flower in your hair. Stand up tall and place your awareness in your feet for a moment so that you are grounded and have a strong foundation.

WHEN YOU FEEL STRONG, LOOK UP AT THE VASTNESS AND POSSIBILITY OF THE SKY AND SAY:

'O Kāne, creator, lord of the light and sky, you who rejected Po, I ask humbly for your assistance.'

POUR THE WATER UPON THE EARTH, THEN AGAIN LOOK UP TO THE SKY AND SAY:

'O Kane, I wish to manifest this [state what it is you wish for] *for myself if it be for my benefit and the benefit of the community as a whole.'*

FACE EAST AND SAY: *'I create here.'*

FACE SOUTH AND SAY: *'I create here.'*

FACE WEST AND SAY: *'I create here.'*

FACE NORTH AND SAY: *'I create here.'*

COME BACK TO YOUR STARTING PLACE, LOOK TO THE SKY AND SAY:

'As I have asked, with your help, Kane, it will be so. I know you require action, not just words. I will commit to doing . . . in your honour.'

FALL

PROGRESSION

The shoulder seasons of fall and spring are often seen as being both easy and hard: easy because they herald some relief from the more extreme summer and winter seasons, but hard because change isn't always easy for the body and mind to accept.

You know rationally that change is universal and you really can't resist it, as to do so makes you rigid in body and mind and you will stop growing and evolving. A much better strategy is to accept change, ride it and utilise the cycle (there is always a cycle) for your own momentum.

Fall is a beautiful season in which the big-push energy of summer disperses a little at first then drops away into a gentler rhythm. While the signs are different depending on where you are geographically, there is generally a change you can see and feel. Obviously the heat of summer gives way and the days grow just that bit shorter. Wind direction changes, our bird friends hunker down or begin their journey to warmer climates and plants begin to slow their growth, having their last go at fruiting and then becoming stagnant again.

THE TRANSFORMATION TREE

This wonderful ritual to perform with your friends can be cast at any time of the lunar phase. Before casting the spell think carefully about where you wish to attract change and transformation within your life; for example, do you want to let go of an old belief, move into a new home that suits you better or step up into a new job? Be specific.

Find a big tree in an open position that attracts breezes and with branches that are low enough for everyone to reach but at least 60 cm from the ground.

Gather three ribbons minimum for each person that are at least 60 cm in length and in fall colours.

Cast a circle or simply welcome the positive energies of the universe or your preferred deity into your space and say out loud:

'I call upon the energies of the changing earth, the cleansing winds and this magnificent tree. We are gathered here in joy and hope, and we thank all that is that we can safely be here together to share intentions for change.'

Each person in turn should hold up their ribbon (one for each wish) and state out loud what it represents and where they want change, although they can do this privately in their mind if they prefer.

After each person expresses this everyone should say:

'I support you. I lend you my energy. May this be so!'

Each person should tie their ribbons to the tree branches so the length of the ribbon hangs down loosely.

Once everyone has tied all their ribbons, thank all the energies that have assisted you and each other.

Let the ribbons fly free and keep watch over them as they eventually fade or the tree loses its leaves. Time will pass and you'll get closer to what you have asked for.

Mabon

FALL EQUINOX, 22 SEPTEMBER, 9.03 PM EDT

An equinox is when the hours of light and dark are equal, a balance that occurs twice a year and is recognised as a sacred time for many cultures. The concept of balance is an important one both in ancient times and possibly even more now.

The equinoxes hold a special place in my heart and this, Mabon, invokes a mightly call for change.

Mabon is the last (or second) harvest festival, an important one that informed those who worked on the land that winter was coming and this was the last chance to harvest and prepare for a leaner time. Seeds would be saved for spring, foods were carefully stored and homes repaired to withstand winter gales.

This equinox would see the whole community coming together to make the best use of the harvest. Although you may not have a smoking house to preserve fish your neighbour would, so your neighbour would smoke your fish or meat. In repayment you would preserve his fruits or make passata or jams from your crops. The last hunting parties would go out, as all too soon game would be hard to find in the snow. Just as with the first harvest festival it was a social time during which news was exchanged and parties arranged.

CELEBRATING MABON

If there is one harvest festival you should get your friends together for it is this one, as it's all about the feast and celebrating the harvest of your life.

What does that mean? Again, it's expressing gratitude for what you have and an understanding of what you have already achieved. You can consider the idea of balance, since it is after all an equinox. Do you burn your candle at both ends or are you not stimulated enough? Is your body in balance? Do you work too hard and not have any fun, or is it the other way around?

My Mabon altar is always a big and robust one featuring freshly baked bread, nuts and seasonal fruits. Another lovely idea is to bake biscuits with one half a dark colour and one half light, symbolising the balance of the elements. The colours featured are bronzes, golds and rich browns.

And a reminder for apiarists: this is a great time to do your last hive checks for the season.

29 Monday

Waxing

30 Tuesday

Waxing

31 Wednesday

Waxing

1 Thursday

Waxing

2 Friday ◐

Waxing

3 Saturday ◐

Waxing

4 Sunday ◐

Waxing

AUGUST							SEPTEMBER						
M	T	W	T	F	S	S	M	T	W	T	F	S	S
1	2	3	4	5	6	7				1	2	3	4
8	9	10	11	12	13	14	5	6	7	8	9	10	11
15	16	17	18	19	20	21	12	13	14	15	16	17	18
22	23	24	25	26	27	28	19	20	21	22	23	24	25
29	**30**	**31**					26	27	28	29	30		

5 Monday ◐

Waxing

6 Tuesday ◐

Waxing

7 Wednesday ◐

Waxing

8 Thursday ◐

Waxing

9 Friday

Waxing

10 Saturday, ◯ full moon in Pisces, 5.59 am EDT

A wonderful night for making aqua luna (moon water). Leave the purest water you can get in a white or silver bowl under the moon and retrieve and bottle prior to dawn. Use this in your spellcraft, your potions and even your bath!

11 Sunday ◗

Waning

You are alive.

Every cell.

Every atom

Glittering in the cosmos.

– THE GODDESS

SEPTEMBER

M	T	W	T	F	S	S
			1	2	3	4
5	6	7	8	9	10	11
12	13	14	15	16	17	18
19	20	21	22	23	24	25
26	27	28	29	30		

12 Monday 🌓

Waning

13 Tuesday 🌓

Waning

14 Wednesday 🌓

Waning

15 Thursday 🌓

Waning

16 Friday ☽

Waning

17 Saturday ☽

Waning

18 Sunday ☽

Waning

SEPTEMBER

M	T	W	T	F	S	S
			1	2	3	4
5	6	7	8	9	10	11
12	**13**	**14**	**15**	**16**	**17**	**18**
19	20	21	22	23	24	25
26	27	28	29	30		

19 Monday ◗

Waning

20 Tuesday ◗

Waning

21 Wednesday ◗

Waning

22 Thursday, ◗ Mabon, fall equinox, 2.33 am EDT

Recognise the harvest of your life and be grateful for what you have. Take stock of what has served you and what has not; let go of what you no longer need and decide to transform for the better.

Waning

23 Friday

Waning

24 Saturday ●

Dark moon.

Embrace the stillness and quiet of the dark moon. A wonderful night to do binding spells.

25 Sunday, ☽ new moon in Libra, 5.54 pm EDT

This is a powerful night to focus on the future. You don't need to keep looking behind you: you aren't going that way.

Allow the wind to play with your hair

Allow the earth to ground your soul

Allow the sun to warm your bones

And the moon to illuminate from within.

– THE GODDESS

SEPTEMBER

M	T	W	T	F	S	S
			1	2	3	4
5	6	7	8	9	10	11
12	13	14	15	16	17	18
19	**20**	**21**	**22**	**23**	**24**	**25**
26	27	28	29	30		

26 Monday

Waxing

27 Tuesday

Waxing

28 Wednesday

Waxing

29 Thursday

Waxing

30 Friday ◑

Waxing

1 Saturday ◑

Waxing

2 Sunday ◑

Waxing

| SEPTEMBER | | | | | | | OCTOBER | | | | | | |
M	T	W	T	F	S	S	M	T	W	T	F	S	S
			1	2	3	4						1	2
5	6	7	8	9	10	11	3	4	5	6	7	8	9
12	13	14	15	16	17	18	10	11	12	13	14	15	16
19	20	21	22	23	24	25	17	18	19	20	21	22	23
26	27	28	29	30			24	25	26	27	28	29	30
							31						

OCTOBER

- What would I like to create, experience and manifest this month?

_____

_____

_____

_____

- What are the important dates for me this month?

_____

_____

- What would give me joy this month?

_____

_____

- What am I devoted to?

_____

_____

- Ideas, musings, actions:

_____

_____

_____

HEKA

GOD OF THE MONTH: OCTOBER

One god was depicted on the walls of many tombs and in many art pieces, but for a long time Egyptologists did not understand who he was. Even though he was pictured somewhat like other gods and he was everywhere, he did not seem to act like other gods. His image was that of a man in royal dress with snakes intertwined either over his head or upon his person around a staff. As there were no temples for this god or offerings found it seemed quite unusual and puzzling.

It was eventually discovered that the mysterious god was Heka and that Heka was, literally, magical. Heka is a force, a movement, an action: if a priest wanted to heal someone he would raise an incantation to Heka (the god) for Heka (the magical force) to heal. Heka's powerful energy could be called upon for all workings. Consider how Maat is the goddess of justice and also the actual force of justice and the universal law itself that runs through all things, which is theoretically close to the idea of Heka's powers.

In the first creation myths Heka was an energy and force at the beginning of all time and at the creation of the universe. He was the force that the god Atum drew upon to create the organised world after stepping from chaos. Heka was woven into every aspect of Egyptian life: birth, death and rebirth but also activities as mundane as eating, cooking and cleaning.

Although misunderstood for a long time, Heka comes to you now as a powerful energy that can assist you in all of your workings.

INCREASING MAGICAL ENERGY SPELL

SOMETIMES YOU MIGHT NEED A MAGICAL BOOST, SO YOU CAN CALL UPON HEKA TO HELP DEVELOP A CLEARER FLOW OF MAGIC. THE BEST TIME TO CAST THE SPELL IS AT A DARK OR FULL MOON.

Draw a snake on one arm and a snake on the other; it doesn't have to be amazing or perfect, just the best you can do.

Gather together:

- a small candle
- resin incense such as frankincense, myrrh, or benzoin
- a pinch of salt
- something made of gold or coated in gold such as a small earring or ring

LIGHT THE CANDLE AND THE INCENSE, SPRINKLE THE SALT ON YOUR FEET AND SAY:

'I am of the earth yet I weave Heka, I call Heka, I flow with Heka. I invoke Heka! I call in my birthright of power and magic. It lives within me and I weave my power with that of Heka.'

TAKE A BREATH, SHUT YOUR EYES AND STAND UP TALL. ENTWINE YOUR ARMS (THUS ENTWINING THE SNAKES DRAWN ON YOUR ARMS) AND SAY:

'Upon the healing serpents of Heka I am Heka, I weave Heka, I fill myself with it. I choose well with my alchemy.'

Visualise the magic snakes curling around you, protecting you and giving you strength. Feel the flow of magic all around and through you, which should feel very powerful and pleasant.

Open your eyes when you are ready, disengage your arms and pick up the gold object.

SAY: *'This is now a talisman of magic and I can use this to remember Heka.'*

Clap three times. If you have any extra magical energy give it to the talisman while holding it or give it back to the earth. Blow out the candle.

Samhain

31 OCTOBER

There is little not to love about Samhain (pronounced 'Sow-en') or, as it's known more popularly, Halloween. It wasn't until I started down the witchcraft path that I learned Halloween wasn't a crazy American festival at all but an ancient Celtic one.

Remember that the Wheel of the Year is linked with the seasons and cycles and their effect on the land, and our ancestors would be experiencing the first bite of winter at Halloween. Everything would be dying back and the fields would fall fallow under snow and ice. Nothing grew then and death hovered and knocked on many doors. Having to eke out a survival-based existence was a genuine situation, while the elderly and sick would suffer from the extremes and perish. Is it any wonder that Samhain became a festival of death – but of death as a part of the cycle of life?

Beltaine, the festival of fertility and life, is opposite on the Wheel of the Year to Samhain.

Samhain, a powerful time full of the magic of our ancestors, teaches us to laugh at death and not fear it, busting our last societal taboos. I always imagine a fallow field in front of me: resting, waiting and ready for the new possibilities I wish to plant within it. Samhain is considered the witches' new year, so happy New Year!

Interestingly, pagans in the southern hemisphere celebrate Halloween on a different date than the usual 31 October because that date isn't the right time seasonally for those on the other side of the world; after all, they would be in spring, not travelling into winter.

CELEBRATING SAMHAIN

One of the most popular traditional activities to do at Samhain is to practise divination. There are two times of the year that the veils between this world and the spirit world are at their thinnest (the other is at Beltaine), which means good-quality oracle work can be done more easily and clear answers are more readily available.

Getting in touch with your ancestors and friends who have passed is another part of Halloween. I love having a wonderful dinner party with lots of beautiful winter foods and fine wine for feasting. We leave the most honoured place, the head of the table, for our 'dead guests', those who this night can join us in spirit and who will be remembered in joy. The honoured dead are served food and wine just as though they were there with us and are included in every aspect of the evening.

It is also a beautiful night to honour those heroes and heroines of the past you have been inspired by. Their spirits live on through your remembering.

3 Monday

Waxing

4 Tuesday

Waxing

5 Wednesday

Waxing

6 Thursday

Waxing

7 Friday ☽

Waxing

8 Saturday ☽

Waxing

9 Sunday, ○ full moon in Aries, 4.54 pm EDT

Take the high road. Do not involve yourself with those with no virtue. Set intentions for peace and ethical power.

OCTOBER
M T W T F S S

					1	2
3	**4**	**5**	**6**	**7**	**8**	**9**
10	11	12	13	14	15	16
17	18	19	20	21	22	23
24	25	26	27	28	29	30
31						

10 Monday ☽

Waning

11 Tuesday ☽

Waning

12 Wednesday ☽

Waning

Wednesday is named after the Norse god Wodin (Odin).

13 Thursday ☽

Waning

14 Friday ◑

Waning

15 Saturday ◑

Waning

16 Sunday ◑

Waning

Wild in your mind

Hot in your heart.

– THE GODDESS

OCTOBER

M	T	W	T	F	S	S
					1	2
3	4	5	6	7	8	9
10	**11**	**12**	**13**	**14**	**15**	**16**
17	18	19	20	21	22	23
24	25	26	27	28	29	30
31						

17 Monday ☽

Waning

18 Tuesday ☽

Waning

19 Wednesday ☽

Waning

20 Thursday ☽

Waning

21 Friday ☽

Waning

22 Saturday ☽

Waning

23 Sunday ☽

Waning

Run free

– THE GODDESS

OCTOBER

M	T	W	T	F	S	S
					1	2
3	4	5	6	7	8	9
10	11	12	13	14	15	16
17	**18**	**19**	**20**	**21**	**22**	**23**
24	25	26	27	28	29	30
31						

OCTOBER

24 Monday

Dark moon.

A night for extreme self-care: stay in, treat yourself beautifully, journal, have a long hot bath.

25 Tuesday, new moon in Scorpio, 6.48 am EDT

This is the perfect time to set intentions for healing of body, mind and spirit.

26 Wednesday ◖

Waxing

27 Thursday ◖

Waxing

This is a good week to remove any unwanted hair as it will grow back more slowly. This week discourages growth.

28 Friday ☽

Waxing

29 Saturday ☽

Waxing

30 Sunday ☽

Waxing

OCTOBER

M	T	W	T	F	S	S
					1	2
3	4	5	6	7	8	9
10	11	12	13	14	15	16
17	18	19	20	21	22	23
24	**25**	**26**	**27**	**28**	**29**	**30**
31						

NOVEMBER

◆ What would I like to create, experience and manifest this month?

_____

_____

_____

_____

◆ What are the important dates for me this month?

_____

_____

◆ What would give me joy this month?

_____

_____

◆ What am I devoted to?

_____

_____

◆ Ideas, musings, actions:

_____

_____

_____

GARUDA

GOD OF THE MONTH: NOVEMBER

Travel was difficult or impossible for the last few years due to the global pandemic, as many countries were locked down. My country, an island nation, was completely shut off to overseas travel for a lengthy amount of time, so travel was on everyone's mind.

As there is a holiday period approaching I wanted to introduce you to a fantastically protective magical being: the god of travel.

Garuda, one of the more ancient Hindu gods, is featured in the Vedas (the oldest scriptures of Hinduism) and in the great epic the Mahābhārata. He is much loved for his assistance to the god Vishnu in a number of his heroic avatars.

The bird-bodied god Garuda was born from a great golden egg. The cosmic shock of the crack lit up the universe, and so powerful was he that all, including the other deities, shook in terror. To make himself more friendly to the gods Garuda reduced his size and energy and flew from heaven to earth to deliver nectar.

A great warrior of huge magical power, Garuda was involved in a battle for the magical potion of eternal life: amrita. While passing a cloud he spotted Vishnu, who as a preserver did not wish to battle with Garuda so suggested that a gentler agreement be reached. Vishnu granted Garuda immortality without the need to drink amrita and Garuda promised to support Vishnu as his flying companion.

From that day forward Garuda aligned himself as Vishnu's magical mount whose speed and agility were key to many of the avatar's victories.

Garuda, still a potent symbol of flight, is the name of Indonesia's national carrier airline. Thailand also uses the Buddhist representation of Garuda as its symbol: a winged deity that can change itself into human form. The idea of a bird going through fire and not only surviving but flourishing, as in the myth of the phoenix, is also closely associated with Garuda's energy.

Call upon Garuda when you are about to undertake a difficult journey or for protection while travelling. If you need to make a connecting flight Garuda will listen to your petition and help you get to the plane on time!

PROTECTION BLESSING FOR TRAVEL

I BLESS MY PASSPORT AND LUGGAGE WHEN I ASK FOR THE PROTECTION OF GARUDA, BUT YOU CAN BLESS ANY TRAVEL-RELATED ITEM.

Cast this spell at the time of a full moon or during the day.

Gather together:
* a red or gold candle
* some incense
* a small feather
* whatever travel-related items you wish blessed

LIGHT THE CANDLE AND SAY:

'Garuda deva, I light this candle in honour of your power and inner fire. I ask that you bless my travels and keep me safe.'

LIGHT THE INCENSE AND PASS THE FEATHER THROUGH THE SMOKE, THEN SAY:

'This feather is a symbol of your speed and might. Please spread your wings around me and protect me upon my journey.'

TOUCH THE FEATHER UPON ALL THE ITEMS YOU WISH TO BLESS AND SAY:

'I bless this in your name, great Garuda.'

When you have completed this, thank Garuda.
Leave the incense and flame burning.
Place the feather somewhere in your luggage or travel documents.

31 Monday ◑

Waxing

It's Samhain: happy witches' new year! It's also a dark moon and time for trick or treat! This is one of the two nights of the year when the veils between the worlds are at their thinnest, so it is a great night for divination of all kinds. Feast with your friends and don't forget those who have passed: set a place for them, pour them wine, leave them delicious food and speak about them.

1 Tuesday ◑

Waxing

2 Wednesday ◑

Waxing

3 Thursday ◑

Waxing

4 Friday

Waxing

5 Saturday

Waxing

6 Sunday

Waxing

OCTOBER								NOVEMBER						
M	T	W	T	F	S	S		M	T	W	T	F	S	S
					1	2		**1**	**2**	**3**	**4**	**5**	**6**	
3	4	5	6	7	8	9		7	8	9	10	11	12	13
10	11	12	13	14	15	16		14	15	16	17	18	19	20
17	18	19	20	21	22	23		21	22	23	24	25	26	27
24	25	26	27	28	29	30		28	29	30				
31														

7 Monday ◐

Waxing

Harvest above-ground fruits and vegetables now.

8 Tuesday, ○ full moon in Taurus, 6.02 am EST

A firm foundation in work and home is important for your peace of mind. Set intentions for comfort, beauty, joy and satisfaction within your work and where you live.

Total lunar eclipse viewable in New York.

9 Wednesday ◑

Waning

10 Thursday ◑

Waning

11 Friday ◗

Waning

12 Saturday ◗

Waning

13 Sunday ◗

Waning

NOVEMBER
M	T	W	T	F	S	S
		1	2	3	4	5	6
7	**8**	**9**	**10**	**11**	**12**	**13**
14	15	16	17	18	19	20
21	22	23	24	25	26	27
28	29	30				

14 Monday 🌘

Waning

15 Tuesday 🌘

Waning

16 Wednesday 🌗

Waning

17 Thursday 🌘

Waning

18 Friday ☽

Waning

19 Saturday ☽

Waning

20 Sunday ☽

Waning

NOVEMBER

M	T	W	T	F	S	S
	1	2	3	4	5	6
7	8	9	10	11	12	13
14	**15**	**16**	**17**	**18**	**19**	**20**
21	22	23	24	25	26	27
28	29	30				

21 Monday

Waning

22 Tuesday

Dark moon.

This is a night to cut cords with relationships that are no longer positive or supporting your well-being.

Harvest below-ground fruits and vegetables now.

23 Wednesday, ☽ new moon in Sagittarius, 5.57 pm EST

Ah! This big bright moon is perfect for casting for new friendships, clients and opportunities. Call in connections of all kinds.

24 Thursday

Trim your hair if you wish to encourage growth.

Waxing

25 Friday ◐

Waxing

26 Saturday ◐

Waxing

27 Sunday ◐

Waxing

NOVEMBER

M	T	W	T	F	S	S
		1	2	3	4	5	6
7	8	9	10	11	12	13
14	15	16	17	18	19	20
21	**22**	**23**	**24**	**25**	**26**	**27**
28	29	30				

DECEMBER

- What would I like to create, experience and manifest this month?

_____

_____

_____

_____

- What are the important dates for me this month?

_____

_____

- What would give me joy this month?

_____

_____

- What am I devoted to?

_____

_____

- Ideas, musings, actions:

_____

_____

_____

BONA DEA

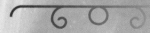

Sometimes when we enter into the darker winter months we tend to also enter into a time of quieter contemplation. We may think about what is working for us and what is not, and we might consider how we got to where we are, our history and our future hopes and dreams.

When we do this it is good to feel safe and secure in our foundation, especially if we are women. I like to work with goddesses that I know will support me in my deeper work, and the ones that are particularly dedicated to women are particularly adept at this assistance. Allow me to suggest one of Rome's original and most powerful goddesses: Bona Dea ('good goddess').

As Bona Dea's worship was partially that of a mystery cult in that the mysteries were tightly held among the worshippers we do not know a great deal about her, but what we do know is that she is old and powerful and is a goddess of and for women. Her temple was in a primary spot on the Aventine Hill and was tended by the famous vestal virgins.

Women of all classes and ages came to worship and leave offerings, although the women who headed or sponsored the rites were often high born or patrician (such as Ceasar's wife). Bona Dea offered protection, justice, fertility and boundaries such as chastity, and the rites included music, dancing, wine and blood sacrifice (normally banned for women in religious practice). She gave women space to be who they were and allowed them an equality that wasn't regularly available under the patriarchal eye of traditional Roman society.

SUPPORT AND PROTECTION RITUAL

I PREFER TO CAST THIS SPELL ON A DARK OR NEW MOON,
BUT ANY TIME YOU NEED IT IS A GOOD TIME.

You'll need:

- a silver or white candle
- incense (myrrh or frankincense is ideal)
- a glass of wine
- a piece of paper and a pen
- a flame-proof bowl

LIGHT THE CANDLE AND SAY:

*'Good mother Bona Dea, you who support and protect women,
I ask you to turn your eyes upon me. I light the flame in your
name. You are the embodiment of the sacred fire.'*

LIGHT THE INCENSE AND SAY:

'I trust this will be pleasant to your senses.'

HOLD UP THE GLASS OF WINE AND SAY:

'I give this gift of the vines as an offering in your name.'

Write down on the paper the area in which you need support.
Fold the paper in half and then in half again.

HOLD IT UP AND SAY:

'Mother Bona Dea, I ask for your support for . . .
[state what is on your paper]. *I release this to you.'*

Burn the paper and place in a flame-proof bowl.

You might wish to ground yourself by eating or drinking something,
having a bath or shower or listening to music with a strong beat.

WINTER

The beauty of quietude

The city in which I live, Sydney in Australia, comes alive in summer. As a city with a world-renowned harbour and many stunning beaches, it fills to the brim in the heat of summer with lots of action and people and socialising. In winter, though, the city changes somewhat: everything slows down and settles, there aren't so many people on the beaches or even tourists in the harbour. The city becomes more introverted, just like the season.

Winter is earth's time to rest and go inward, a time for growth to pause (although it never completely ceases). You can reflect on this inclination and slow down too; you can plan, dream, dawdle, spend time inside cooking or cocooning and catch up on things you may have missed with the speed and intensity of the prior months.

Winter can be a period during which you spend more time with yourself. Solitude isn't loneliness; it simply means you spend time without the chaos and influence of others so you can think and plan and create on your own unimpeded by others. Depending on where you live winter can be extreme, which means you can fully immerse yourself in the sensory power of the season. Cold and all the simplicity that it brings can be so beautiful, especially if you have the right clothing!

Winter is also the perfect time to work with underworld gods and goddesses and those who reign over mountains, ice and snow. These wonderful energies are often very welcome associates who help us navigate through a difficult obstacle or leave behind a past that wasn't so positive. Allow me to recommend Nuit, Hekate, Osiris, Persephone, Maat, Hel, Skaði or Ull.

FIREPIT-CLEARING SPELL

I love to do this spell using our small firepit but you can do it with any open fire or even a small fire within your cast-iron cauldron. It's perfect to do either with friends or solo. Before casting the spell, consider what aspects of your experience you want to get rid of; useful examples are fears, burdens, misunderstandings, imbalances or bad habits.

Make sure everyone present is comfortable. Set the fire and get it well established. Give everyone a piece of log or branch to burn and get them to write on their wood what they wish to get clear of. This can be represented as words or symbols. When everyone has done this say:

'Season of winter, loving universe, great element of fire: thank you for your energy! We are being warmed by your presence. Thank you.'

Focus on what the fire looks and smells like and feel the heat. One by one, speak of what you wish to be released. Everyone should witness this and be supportive. When the person speaking is ready they should toss their wood with the words or symbols onto the fire and say:

'I release this to the fire. Gone, gone, gone: it is no more!'

When it is all done, loudly clap three times. So it will be as you have asked!

Yule, the winter solstice

21 DECEMBER, 4.48 PM EST

There are three enduring symbols of Yule: the Yule tree (bringing nature inside); gift giving (representing the joy of surviving another season and gratitude for fecundity returning); and the Yule log (which is covered in wishes for the future and ritually burnt). The highly magical ashes can be used in other workings later in the year.

It's easy to see the similarities with Christmas and in Europe Yule is tied closely to Christmas, although Christmas celebrations are actually referred to as Yule (or Yul) celebrations in some areas. However, Yule is a pre-Christian celebration so Christmas certainly has Yule DNA.

Yule is a solstice festival, which means we observe where we are in the cycle of light and dark. It celebrates the return of the light after the longest night of the year, highlighting the idea of a birth of light and hope over darkness as from this night onwards the daylight hours will grow by a tiny increment each day and the warmth will return to the earth.

Why is this a cause for celebration? Imagine how tough our ancestors would have had it in the depth of winter: no reliable heating, and no supermarkets or shopping centres and scarce food supplies with no hot and easy takeaway. Imagine how much you would look forward to some relief from the scarcity and hardship with longer daylight hours and more sun.

CELEBRATING YULE

Many witches make handmade or hand-grown presents for their family and friends. I make potions, bath salts and talismans with tones of magic and gratitude for my loved ones. I decorate my altar with greens and golds, lots of sparkly candles and sweet incense such as frankincense, pine and myrrh. I make a powerful spiced mulled wine and Yule cookies with little fortunes written in piped icing sugar on the bottom side.

The important Yule log should preferably be a branch or section of wood that a tree has discarded, but if you have firewood then choose a nice piece. Prepare some small slips of paper for yourself and your guests to write their hopeful wishes upon. Really consider these carefully as this is a powerfully magical night for wish manifestation. Do not waste it!

Pin the wishes on the log or cut slits into the log so that the wood clips the slips like a wooden paperclip. Start a fire in a hearth or fire pit and stoke it so it is roaring. Add your log to the flames for its hopeful transformation. Everyone can sing or speak aloud their wishes or hopes of something new to replace the old.

28 Monday ◑

Waxing

29 Tuesday ◑

Waxing

30 Wednesday ◑

Waxing

1 Thursday ◑

Waxing

2 Friday 🌓

Waxing

3 Saturday 🌓

Waxing

4 Sunday 🌓

Waxing

Somewhere someone is experiencing their best day ever.

Somewhere someone is experiencing their worst day ever.

Most of us are in the arc in between.

All this too shall pass.

- THE GODDESS

NOVEMBER						
M	T	W	T	F	S	S
	1	2	3	4	5	6
7	8	9	10	11	12	13
14	15	16	17	18	19	20
21	22	23	24	25	26	27
28	**29**	**30**				

DECEMBER						
M	T	W	T	F	S	S
			1	**2**	**3**	**4**
5	6	7	8	9	10	11
12	13	14	15	16	17	18
19	20	21	22	23	24	25
26	27	28	29	30	31	

5 Monday ◑

Waxing

6 Tuesday ◑

Waxing

7 Wednesday, ○ full moon in Gemini, 11.08 pm EST

Enjoy the last full moon of 2022, a moon to set intentions for courage, resilience and personal power!

8 Thursday ◐

Waning

9 Friday ☽

Waning

10 Saturday ☽

Waning

11 Sunday ☽

Waning

Be fully alive

As I have made you

Experiencing all.

- THE GODDESS

DECEMBER

M	T	W	T	F	S	S
			1	2	3	4
5	6	7	8	9	10	11
12	13	14	15	16	17	18
19	20	21	22	23	24	25
26	27	28	29	30	31	

12 Monday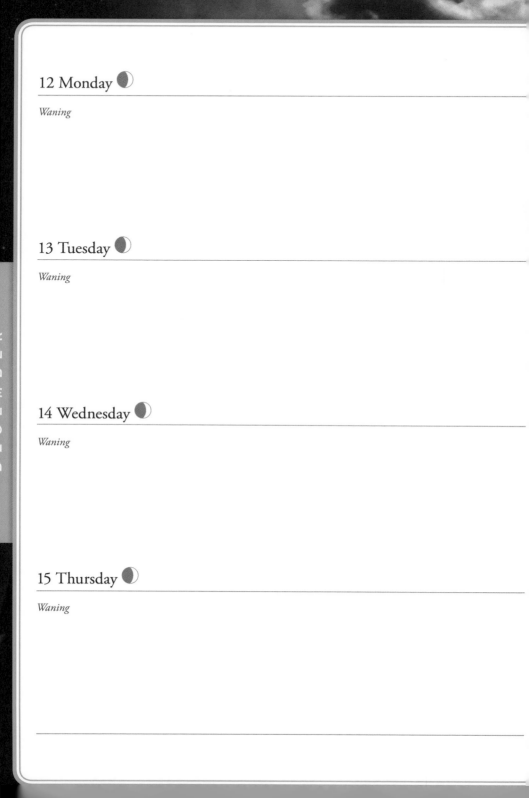

Waning

13 Tuesday

Waning

14 Wednesday

Waning

15 Thursday

Waning

16 Friday ◗

Waning

17 Saturday ◗

Waning

18 Sunday ◗

Waning

Your body is the instrument of your soul

Take care of it, love it, for it is sacred.

- THE GODDESS

DECEMBER

M	T	W	T	F	S	S
			1	2	3	4
5	6	7	8	9	10	11
12	**13**	**14**	**15**	**16**	**17**	**18**
19	20	21	22	23	24	25
26	27	28	29	30	31	

19 Monday

Waning

20 Tuesday

Waning

21 Wednesday Yule, the winter solstice, 4.48 pm EST

Waning

Happy Yule! This solstice reflects the shortest day of the year and the longest night, when hope breaks through the darkness. It is a traditional feasting time and one of the best times to make charms and talismans for abundance. Make delicious mulled wine and burn a Yule log that has your wishes attached to it.

22 Thursday

Dark moon

23 Friday, new moon in Capricorn, 5.16 am EST

This is the perfect night for planning a new strategy for next year.
Super new moon.

24 Saturday

Waxing
Christmas Eve.

25 Sunday

Waxing
Christmas Day.

Be friends with other species

The furred, the finned, the feathered.

All have their wisdom for you.

- THE GODDESS

DECEMBER

M	T	W	T	F	S	S
			1	2	3	4
5	6	7	8	9	10	11
12	13	14	15	16	17	18
19	**20**	**21**	**22**	**23**	**24**	**25**
26	27	28	29	30	31	

D E C E M B E R

26 Monday

Waxing

27 Tuesday

Waxing

28 Wednesday

Waxing

29 Thursday

Waxing

30 Friday ◐

Waxing

31 Saturday ◐

Waxing

The last night of the year, so catch the positive wave of the power of the new year! Mark the moment with a kiss, a dance or a sip of champagne. Spill a little on the ground for Jana, the goddess of the new year.

Look for Stacey Demarco on Facebook for the free annual Ride the Wave Ritual Event. Let go of what was, ready yourself for new momentum and ensure you have your intentions set for 2023! Mark the end of this year with a ritual of gratitude before you head out to celebrate. At midnight, connect with the wave of new hope and know that your resolutions will come to fruition!

1 Sunday ◐   January 2023

Waxing

Welcome to 2023!

DECEMBER							JANUARY 2023						
M	T	W	T	F	S	S	M	T	W	T	F	S	S
			1	2	3	4							1
5	6	7	8	9	10	11	2	3	4	5	6	7	8
12	13	14	15	16	17	18	9	10	11	12	13	14	15
19	20	21	22	23	24	25	16	17	18	19	20	21	22
26	27	28	29	30	31		23	24	25	26	27	28	29
							30	31					

NOTES AND MUSINGS

REORDER FOR 2023 LUNAR DIARY

Name..

Address..

City...State..................

Postcode....................Country........................

Phone..

Email..

Mastercard ☐   Visa ☐

Credit card number...

Name on card...

Expiry date: ....CVV number...............

Please send me .... copies of

2023 Lunar Diary

$29.99 per copy

Send to:
Rockpool Publishing
PO Box 252
Summer Hill NSW 2130
Phone 61 2 9560 1280
www.rockpoolpublishing.co

For trade orders:
Simon and Schuster Australia
Phone 02 9983 6600
cservice@simonandschuster.com.au

2022 MOON PHASES:

UNIVERSAL TIME CHART

Below is a handy chart that gives moon phases in universal time (UT). It is the mean solar time for the meridian at Greenwich, England, and is used as the basis for calculating time throughout most of the world.

DARK MOON	NEW MOON	FULL MOON
1 January	2 January, 6.33 pm	17 January, 11.48 pm
31 January	1 February, 5.46 pm	16 February, 4.56 pm
1 March	2 March, 5.34 pm	18 March, 7.17 am
31 March	1 April, 6.24 am	16 April, 6.55 pm
29 April	30 April, 8.28 pm	16 May, 4.14 am
29 May	30 May, 11.30 am	14 June, 11.51 am
28 June	29 June, 2.52 am	13 July, 6.37 pm
27 July	28 July, 5.54 pm	12 August, 1.35 am
26 August	27 August, 8.17 am	10 September, 9.59 am
24 September	25 September, 9.54 pm	9 October, 8.54 pm
24 October	25 October, 10.48 am	8 November, 11.02 am
22 November	23 November, 10.57 pm	8 December, 4.08 am
22 December	23 December, 10.16 am	

RESOURCES

Below is a list of handy moon, earth and pagan-related resources that I particularly like, and if you are interested there are many fan pages for gods and goddesses you can join.

www.paganawareness.net.au: If you want more information on paganism or witchcraft this is a great place to start. Pagan Awareness Network Australia Inc. (PAN) is a not-for-profit educational association with members Australia-wide. It is directed by a management committee whose  members are drawn from a broad cross section of the pagan community. It has no formal ties with any religious body and works proactively both within the pagan community and as a point of contact for the public, including government and media organisations. PAN aims to continue as the Australian pagan community's most effective networking and educational body.

www.themodernwitch.com: My website contains loads of free resources and downloads and witches' tools and is a store from which you can obtain books, downloads, blessed talismans and temple beads, including lunar beads. Register for the free newsletter!

www.natureluster.com: This is my site about the benefits and wonders of an earth-centred life. Try the Natureluster Programme.

You can also find Natureluster on Instagram.

LUNAR WEBSITES

- *http://eclipse.gsfc.nasa.gov/phase/phasecat.html*: this NASA site provides historical and current information about moon phases. It is wonderful for researching your lunar return.
- *www.timeanddate.com*: this website is great for lunar timing and equinox information.

TIDAL INFORMATION

Strangely enough, some of the best tidal information comes from popular newspapers. Check your state.

MOON GARDENING

For moon gardening check out *www.green-change.com* or *www.moongardeningcalendar.com*.

FACEBOOK/INSTAGRAM

Connect with me on Facebook: *http://www.facebook.com/staceydemarco* or look for The Modern Witch on Instagram.

ABOUT THE AUTHOR

Stacey Demarco, the Modern Witch, is passionate about bringing practical magic to everyone and inspiring people to have a deeper connection with nature.

Stacey has been teaching for more than 20 years and is the author of the best-sellers *Witch in the Boardroom*, *Witch in the Bedroom* and *The Enchanted Moon* (Oct 2021), which have been translated into many other languages. She is the co-writer of *The No Excuses Guide to Soulmates*, *The No Excuses Guide to Purpose* and *Plants of Power*. Her oracle card decks include the best-selling *Queen of the Moon Oracle*, *Divine Animals Oracle* and *The Elemental Oracle,* all illustrated by Kinga Britschgi.

She is the founder of Natureluster, which educates and works to reconnect people with the health-giving power of nature.

Stacey is an animal activist, ethical beekeeper and dedicated adventure traveller who lives by the beach in Sydney with her husband and furry companions. She provides private consultations, conducts workshops and leads the popular Wild Souls naturelusting retreats nationally and internationally. You can learn more at www.themodernwitch.com.